Sexual Orientation and Gender Identity Discrimination

Comparative Discrimination Law

Volumes published in this Brill Research Perspective are listed at *brill.com/rpcd*

Sexual Orientation and Gender Identity Discrimination

By

Holning Lau

BRILL

LEIDEN | BOSTON

This paperback book edition is simultaneously published as issue 2.2 (2018) of *Comparative Discrimination Law*, DOI:10.1163/24522031-12340004.

Library of Congress Control Number: 2018950591

Typeface for the Latin, Greek, and Cyrillic scripts: "Brill". See and download: brill.com/brill-typeface.

ISBN 978-90-04-34548-5 (paperback)
ISBN 978-90-04-34549-2 (e-book)

This book is printed on acid-free paper and produced in a sustainable manner.

Contents

Sexual Orientation and Gender Identity Discrimination

Holning Lau
Willie P. Mangum Distinguished Professor of Law
University of North Carolina School of Law
hslau@email.unc.edu

Abstract

Laws concerning sexual orientation and gender identity (SOGI) have undergone a sea change. Still, legal protections against SOGI discrimination vary widely around the world. As jurisdictions wrestle with whether and how to protect people against SOGI discrimination, several conceptual questions emerge. This Brill volume reviews and discusses legal developments and scholarly commentary concerning these questions. Specifically, this volume examines the following five questions: (1) Is SOGI discrimination encompassed by existing laws prohibiting discrimination based on sex? (2) Should sexual orientation and gender identity be considered protected categories in and of themselves? (3) Is there a standard sequence of steps for developing legal protections against SOGI discrimination? (4) What are the drawbacks of developing SOGI discrimination protections? (5) To what extent should religious objections justify exemptions from SOGI discrimination bans?

Keywords

discrimination – equality – comparative – sexual orientation – gender identity – LGBT – LGBTI – SOGI – SOGISC – SOGIESC – Toonen – Obergefell – Fourie

 | DOI:10.1163/9789004345492_002

Introduction

Laws concerning sexual orientation[1] and gender identity[2] (SOGI) have undergone a sea change. Many jurisdictions around the world have repealed their laws that criminalized same-sex intimacy and expression of diverse gender identities. In addition, a growing number of jurisdictions are further reforming their laws to protect lesbian, gay, bisexual, and transgender (LGBT) persons against discrimination. Legal regimes at various levels—international, regional, national, and subnational—have deemed SOGI discrimination to be impermissible in contexts ranging from employment and housing to marriage and parenting.[3]

Developments at the United Nations reflect the globalization of SOGI rights. The United Nations Office of the High Commissioner of Human Rights has made combatting SOGI discrimination a priority, as demonstrated by its "Free and Equal" campaign aimed at cultivating SOGI rights.[4] Likewise, the United Nations Human Rights Council passed a historic resolution in 2016, appointing the United Nations' first-ever Independent Expert on protection against violence and discrimination based on sexual orientation and gender identity.[5]

Despite these developments, legal protections around the world remain fragmented. In many countries, LGBT persons continue to suffer persecution

1 This volume adopts the definition of "sexual orientation" found in the Yogyakarta Principles in Relation to Sexual Orientation and Gender Identity (Yogyakarta Principles): "Sexual orientation is understood to refer to each person's capacity for profound emotional, affectional and sexual attraction to, and intimate and sexual relations with, individuals of a different gender or the same gender or more than one gender." A group of distinguished human rights experts launched the Yogyakarta Principles as a non-binding interpretation of states' human rights obligations concerning sexual orientation and gender identity. Although human rights treaties do not explicitly address sexual orientation or gender identity, the Yogyakarta Principles apply generic treaty provisions to issues concerning sexual orientation and gender identity. See Yogyakarta Principles (2007), at 6, and Yogyakarta Principles Plus Ten (2017), both available at yogyakartaprinciples.org.

2 According to the Yogyakarta Principles: "Gender identity is understood to refer to each person's deeply felt internal and individual experience of gender, which may or may not correspond with the sex assigned at birth, including the personal sense of the body (which may involve, if freely chosen, modification of bodily appearance or function by medical, surgical or other means) and other expressions of gender, including dress, speech and mannerisms." Yogyakarta Principles, supra note 1, at 6.

3 Dominic McGoldrick, "The Development and Status of Sexual Orientation Discrimination under International Human Rights Law," 16 *Human Rights Law Review* 613 (2016).

4 See United Nations Human Rights Office, *About UN Free & Equal*, www.unfe.org/about.

5 United Nations Human Rights Council, *Resolution Adopted by the Human Rights Council on 30 June 2016*, UN Doc. A/HRC/RES/32/2.

and have no legal recourse.[6] Countries that do protect against SOGI discrimination do so to varying degrees and have based their protections on divergent legal theories. Indeed, numerous conceptual debates have emerged over the course of law reform. This volume provides an overview of how various legal institutions and commentators around the world have contributed to these debates. With its distillation of these debates, this volume serves as a guide for researchers who seek to acquaint themselves with comparative approaches to SOGI discrimination law.

This volume proceeds in six steps. Part I lays the groundwork by clarifying terminology, scope, and methodology. Parts II and III then examine the debates about how sexual orientation and gender identity fit into discrimination law's framework of protected categories. Some jurisdictions refer to these "protected categories" as "prohibited grounds of discrimination," and this volume will use the two phrases interchangeably. Part II examines whether SOGI discrimination should be considered sex discrimination and thus be covered by existing laws that regard sex as a protected category. Part III then considers whether sexual orientation and gender identity should be protected categories in and of themselves.

Protections against SOGI discrimination have developed incrementally. Part IV examines the nature of this incrementalism. LGBT persons experience discrimination in a range of contexts including the criminal system, employment, housing, public accommodations, marriage, and parenting. Governments historically have not reformed their laws to address these various areas all at once. Instead, governments tend to expand incrementally the range of contexts in which they prohibit SOGI discrimination. Part IV addresses whether there is a typical sequence to such incremental law reform. Part IV also examines another type of incrementalism: some jurisdictions are leaders in law reform and then other jurisdictions follow. This relationship among jurisdictions is discussed in Part IV.

The final two Parts of this volume explore the limits of SOGI discrimination laws. Part V examines critiques from progressive commentators who believe that SOGI nondiscrimination protections have significant drawbacks. Part VI then discusses ongoing debates about whether and how SOGI discrimination bans should include exemptions for religious objectors. The volume then

---

6 See, e.g., Vitit Muntarbhorn (as United Nations Independent Expert on protection against violence and discrimination based on sexual orientation and gender identity), "Protection Against Violence and Discrimination Based on Sexual Orientation and Gender Identity," UN Doc. A/72/172 (17 July 2017).

concludes by reflecting on how this volume illuminates the value of studying SOGI discrimination law from comparative perspectives.

I Terminology, Scope, and Methodology

This volume uses several terms that are worth explaining. It refers to individuals with a minority sexual orientation or gender identity through the commonly used acronym LGBT, which stands for "lesbian, gay, bisexual, and transgender."[7] In other words, the term "LGBT" describes people who are non-heterosexual and/or non-cisgender.

One shortcoming of this term is the fact that individuals who have a minority sexual orientation or gender identity may not self-identify as LGBT. Indeed, in some parts of the world, local terminology for SOGI identity categories captures nuance or fluidity that the LGBT acronym erases; local identity labels may also be imbued with cultural significance that is lost when replaced by the LGBT acronym.[8] For economy of language, however, this volume will use the acronym LGBT, which has become commonplace in English-language legal literature. It will also use the phrase "SOGI minorities" when emphasizing that not all individuals with a minority sexual orientation or gender identity identify as LGBT.

One might question why issues of sexual orientation and gender identity are discussed in tandem, given that an individual's sexual orientation and gender identity are distinguishable. Indeed, whether someone is lesbian, gay, bisexual, or straight is not necessarily related to whether the individual is transgender or cisgender. Notwithstanding distinctions between sexual orientation and gender identity, the two are closely linked in culture and politics. Discrimination based on sexual orientation and discrimination based on gender identity often stem from a shared root: the social policing of gender norms.[9] For example, in many parts of the world, lesbians and transgender women are both perceived as violating socially constructed expectations about what it means to be a woman. Although transgender women breach gender norms through their gender identity, and lesbians breach gender norms through their sexual

7 When speaking specifically about sexual orientation and not gender identity, this volume will refer to LGB persons, as opposed to LGBT persons.

8 See, e.g., Inter-American Commission on Human Rights, *Violence Against LGBTI Persons* 26–27 (2015) (discussing SOGI identity labels, such as "Muxe" in Mexico and "Mati" in Suriname, that do not fit neatly within the LGBT acronym); Holning Lau et al., "Assessing the Tongzhi Label: Self-Identification and Public Opinion," 64 *Journal of Homosexuality* 509 (2017) (discussing the Chinese term "tongzhi").

9 This point will be discussed in further detail in Part II.

orientation, both are perceived as violating norms regarding what it means to be a woman.

There is also a long history of coalitional politics among sexual orientation and gender identity minorities. To be sure, the strength of LGBT coalitions has fluctuated over time and place, but such coalitions have had lasting influence on advocacy and law reform.[10] For example, the previously mentioned United Nations Independent Expert is tasked with working on issues of sexual orientation as well as gender identity.[11]

Intersex issues also frequently interact with LGBT issues. As LGBT persons are targets of discrimination because they breach cultural expectations about "manhood" and "womanhood," prejudice is also directed at intersex persons because their bodies do not conform to social expectations for what it means to be a man or woman. Accordingly, human rights defenders often consider intersex issues alongside LGBT issues. This is reflected in the growing use of the acronyms LGBTI (with the "I" standing for "intersex") and SOGISC (with the "SC" standing for "sex characteristics"). Likewise, in 2017 when human rights experts updated the Yogyakarta Principles, which were originally a statement about LGBT rights, they added recommendations pertaining to intersex rights.[12] Despite the relationship between SOGI discrimination and intersex discrimination, this volume will focus on SOGI discrimination. Because legal developments concerning intersex issues are relatively nascent, they warrant fuller treatment in a volume of their own.

This volume approaches SOGI discrimination as a general topic, as opposed to focusing on discrimination in any specific context such as employment, education, or family life. In examining the regulation of discrimination, this volume considers law at a variety of levels, from international to national and subnational. In doing so, the volume does not seek to provide a comprehensive survey of laws around the world. Instead, it selectively chooses examples to illustrate different approaches to developing protections against SOGI discrimination. This volume aims to offer comparative insights on pathways for developing protections against SOGI discrimination. Thus, it focuses on

10 See, e.g., Jena McGill, "SOGI ... So What: Sexual Orientation, Gender Identity and Human Rights Discourse at the United Nations," 3 *Canadian Journal of Human Rights* 1, 23–25 (2014) (discussing the relationship between sexual orientation and gender identity in international human rights advocacy); Shannon Minter, "Do Transsexuals Dream of Gay Rights? Getting Real about Transgender Inclusion in the Gay Rights Movement," 17 *New York Law School Journal of Human Rights* 589 (2000–2001) (discussing the LGBT coalition in the United States).

11 United Nations Human Rights Council, supra note 5.

12 Yogyakarta Principles Plus Ten, supra note 1.

jurisdictions that have in fact developed such protections instead of the jurisdictions where no such protections exist.

II SOGI Discrimination as Sex Discrimination

The legal principle of nondiscrimination does not prohibit all forms of discrimination. Instead, it dictates that discrimination based on certain grounds—also known as protected categories—is presumed impermissible. Sex has long been considered a protected category in discrimination law. Human rights treaties and a broad range of national laws around the world either state explicitly that sex is a protected category or have been interpreted by courts as such.[13]

A question that continues to be debated is whether SOGI discrimination is a form of sex discrimination. This question has been particularly salient in jurisdictions such as the United States, where Congress has refused to pass legislation that expressly prohibits SOGI discrimination.[14] Because of this legislative gap, individuals who have suffered discrimination based on sexual orientation or gender identity have sought to persuade courts that the discrimination they suffered is prohibited by longstanding bans of sex discrimination.

The remainder of this Part is divided into three sections. First, the following section describes legal theories supporting the claim that sexual orientation discrimination is a form of sex discrimination. The second section articulates legal theories for why gender identity discrimination is a type of sex discrimination. The third section examines objections to viewing prohibitions of sex discrimination as subsuming prohibitions of SOGI discrimination.

---

13 See, e.g., Mpoki Mwakagali, "International Human Rights Law and Discrimination Protections: A Comparison of Regional and National Responses," 1 *Comparative Discrimination Law* 1 (2017) (discussing numerous international treaties that list sex as a protected category); UN Women, *Gender Equality and Women's Empowerment: Constitutional Jurisprudence* (2017) (discussing constitutional regulation of sex discrimination).

14 Although the US Congress has not passed legislation to ban sexual orientation discrimination at the federal level, 22 states within the United States and the District of Columbia have statutes that prohibit sexual orientation-based employment discrimination. See Movement Advancement Project, *Non-Discrimination Laws*, www.lgbtmap.org/equality-maps/non_discrimination_laws (data current as of 29 March 2018). The US Supreme Court has also interpreted the federal Constitution to prohibit certain forms of sexual orientation discrimination, but the Constitution does not apply to private actors, and the extent of the Constitution's protection against sexual orientation discrimination in the public sector remains unclear. See Nan D. Hunter, "Interpreting Liberty and Equality Through the Lens of Marriage," 6 *California Law Review Circuit* 107, 113–114 (2015).

II.A *Sexual Orientation*

In the landmark 1994 case of *Toonen v. Australia*, the United Nations Human Rights Committee endorsed the idea that discrimination based on sexual orientation is a form of sex discrimination.[15] Gay rights activist Nicholas Toonen had challenged the criminal prohibition of homosexual sexual activity in Tasmania. The Human Rights Committee held that the law in question violated privacy and nondiscrimination rights enshrined in the International Covenant on Civil and Political Rights (ICCPR). The ICCPR lists certain protected categories. Sexual orientation does not appear on that list, but the ICCPR does explicitly name "sex" as a protected category.[16] In *Toonen*, the Human Rights Committee stated that "the reference to 'sex' [as a prohibited ground of discrimination] ... is to be taken as including sexual orientation."[17] Accordingly, Tasmania's law amounted to sex discrimination because it targeted homosexual activity but not heterosexual activity.

Through *Toonen*, the UN Human Rights Committee became one of a few tribunals at the vanguard of accepting the notion that sexual orientation discrimination is a form of sex discrimination.[18] The *Toonen* opinion offered no analysis, however, to explain the relationship between sexual orientation and sex discrimination.

Subsequent tribunals, as well as scholarly commentary, have gone a long way in filling that gap. The United States is an apt case study because it has produced a considerably large jurisprudence on this topic. The United States Equal Employment Opportunity Commission (EEOC) has provided one of the clearest articulations of the conceptualization of sexual orientation discrimination being a form of sex discrimination. The EEOC offered this explanation in the case of *Baldwin v. Foxx*.[19] David Baldwin was a gay man who worked as an air traffic controller at Miami International Airport. He held a temporary position and was denied a permanent position when it became available. Baldwin argued that his supervisor rejected him for the permanent position because the supervisor disapproved of his sexual orientation. In addressing this

15 Toonen v. Australia, UN Doc. CCPR/C/50/D/488/1992 (4 April 1994).

16 International Covenant on Civil and Political Rights (ICCPR), Art. 26.

17 Toonen, supra note 15, at para. 8.6.

18 The UN Human Rights Committee decided *Toonen* in 1994. The previous year, the Hawaii Supreme Court ruled in its landmark same-sex marriage case that sexual orientation discrimination is inherently a type of sex discrimination that receives strict scrutiny according to the Hawaiian constitution. Baehr v. Lewin, 852 P.2d 44, 64–67 (1993) (plurality opinion). That same year, an appellate court in California held that discrimination against a same-sex couple amounted to sex discrimination. Engel v. Worthington, 23 Cal. Rptr. 2d 329 (Ct. App. 1993).

19 Baldwin v. Foxx, EEOC Appeal No. 0120133080, 2015 WL 4397641 (15 July 2015).

claim, the EEOC needed to determine whether the United States' federal ban on employment discrimination, Title VII of the 1964 Civil Rights Act (Title VII), prohibits discrimination based on sexual orientation. Like the ICCPR, Title VII does not explicitly address sexual orientation. It does, however, list sex as a protected category.[20] Thus, the EEOC needed to evaluate whether the prohibition of sex discrimination subsumes a prohibition of sexual orientation discrimination.

The EEOC answered in the affirmative and offered a lengthy explanation for why sexual orientation is a type of sex discrimination. This explanation can be broken down into two main rationales, which I will call the definitional and stereotyping rationales. According to the first rationale, a person's sexual orientation is necessarily defined via reference to the person's sex.[21] Thus, an employer who discriminates against an employee based on sexual orientation is necessarily treating that employee differently based on sex. Consider the example of an employer who punishes a gay man for displaying a photo of his boyfriend on his desk, while allowing female colleagues to display photos of their boyfriends.[22] The employer is discriminating against the gay man because of his sexual orientation, and his sexual orientation is defined by reference to his sex. If the employee were not a man, his display of affection toward a boyfriend would not have provoked the employer's ire. In this way, sexual orientation discrimination is always a form of sex discrimination.

To further illustrate the definitional rationale, the EEOC drew a comparison to earlier race discrimination cases called "associational discrimination" cases.[23] US courts have held that if an employer discriminates against a white employee for being in an interracial relationship, that discrimination amounts to racial discrimination. This is so because the employer must take into account the employee's race to determine that the employee is in an interracial relationship. Likewise, an employer who discriminates against individuals in same-sex relationships must take into account an employee's sex to determine whether the employee is in a same-sex relationship. In other words, the employee's relationship is defined by reference to the employee's sex.

The EEOC also explained that discrimination based on sexual orientation counts as discrimination based on sex stereotyping.[24] According to Title VII case law, if an employer treats an employee adversely because the employee

20 Title VII of the Civil Rights Act of 1964 ("Title VII"), 42 U.S.C. Secs. 2000e, et seq. (United States).

21 Baldwin, supra note 19, at 7–8.

22 Cf. id. at 7.

23 Id. at 8–9.

24 Id. at 9–11.

failed to conform to sex stereotypes, that adverse treatment would constitute sex discrimination. The EEOC explained that the idea that "real men" are attracted to women, and "real women" are attracted to men, is essentially a stereotype. Thus, if an employer rejects an employee for being homosexual, that rejection is based on sex stereotypes and amounts to sex discrimination. This stereotyping rationale and the definitional rationale coexist; both of them link sexual orientation discrimination with sex discrimination.

While *Baldwin* was a case about employment discrimination, its logic can be applied to sexual orientation discrimination in other areas of life, such as education and marriage. With that said, the EEOC's rulings are not binding on US courts, and US federal circuit courts are currently split on whether Title VII's ban on sex discrimination subsumes a prohibition of sexual orientation discrimination.[25] The US Supreme Court may eventually address this circuit split. Courts in the United Kingdom and the European Court of Justice have also refused to apply sex discrimination bans to sexual orientation discrimination.[26] Part II.C will examine some of the objections to the argument that sexual orientation discrimination is a form of sex discrimination.

II.B *Gender Identity*

Courts and government agencies have wrestled with whether discrimination based on gender identity is a form of sex discrimination. In the United States, a sizeable number of courts and administrative agencies have decided that gender identity discrimination is in fact a form of sex discrimination;[27] however, the question is not yet completely settled in the United States.[28] Some courts in Europe and Asia have also endorsed the view that prohibitions of sex discrimination encompass gender identity discrimination.[29] Drawing on

25 For cases ruling that sexual orientation discrimination is a form of sex discrimination, see Zarda, v. Altitude Express, 883 F.3d 100 (2nd Cir. 2018) (en banc); Hively v. Ivy Tech Community College of Indiana, 853 F.3d 339 (7th Cir. 2017) (en banc). For a case rejecting this position, see Evans v. Georgia Regional Hospital, 850 F.3d 1248 (11th Cir.), cert. denied, 138 S. Ct. 557 (2017).

26 See Macdonald v. Advocate General for Scotland, SLT 1158 (2003); Shirley P. Pearce v. Governing Body of Mayfield School, 2001 WL 825287 (Ct. App., 31 July 2001); Regina v. Secretary of State for Defence, ex parte Perkins, 1 FLR 491 (1999); Grant v. South-West Trains Ltd., All ER 193 (1998); Smith v. Gardner Merchant Ltd., IRLR 342 (1996); Regina v. Ministry of Defence, ex parte Smith, 4 All ER 427 (1995).

27 See Katie Eyer, "Sex Discrimination Law and LGBT Equality," *ACS Issue Brief*, August 2017, at 5, n.19 (listing US cases).

28 See id. at 11–12.

29 See National Legal Services Authority (NALSA) v. Union of India, SCC 1 (India 2014); P v. S & Cornwall City Council, Case C-13/94 [1996] ECR 1–2143 (ECJ). See also Isabelle

illustrative cases from around the world, this section identifies three rationales for this view. This volume will refer to them as the stereotyping, transition, and categorical rationales.

The stereotyping rationale applies to gender identity much like it applies to sexual orientation, as discussed previously. Disapproval of transgender people can be understood as disapproval of people who challenge sex stereotypes. For example, an employer may perceive a male-to-female transgender individual as violating stereotypes about manhood because the individual dresses as a woman. Similarly, the employer may also perceive the individual as breaching stereotypes about womanhood because the individual is perceived as being insufficiently feminine. In this regard, discrimination against transgender individuals is a form of sex discrimination. In the United States, the EEOC and numerous federal appellate courts have adopted this rationale.[30] Likewise, in a landmark case protecting transgender rights, the Supreme Court of India stated that discrimination "for the reason of not being in conformity with stereotypical generalizations of binary genders" constituted sex discrimination.[31]

Discrimination that targets people who transition from one sex to another is also a form of sex discrimination. One US federal court, in the case of *Schroer v. Billington*, explained this by analogizing to religion.[32] If an employer does not discriminate against Christians or Muslims, but fires an employee for converting from Christianity to Islam, that would constitute religious discrimination under US law. By analogy, even if an employer does not discriminate against men or women, the employer discriminates based on sex if the employer fires an employee for transitioning from being a man to being a woman. The European Court of Justice (ECJ) also seemed to embrace a version of this transition rationale. *In P v. S and Cornwall City Council*, the ECJ held that an employer had committed sex discrimination by treating an employee unfavorably because of the employee's plans to undergo sex reassignment.[33] Although

Chopin & Catharina Germaine, European Commission, *A Comparative Analysis of Non-discrimination Law in Europe 2017*, at 33 (2017) (noting that discrimination laws in Austria and the Netherlands treat discrimination against transgender persons as sex discrimination).

30 See, e.g., Whitaker v. Kenosha Unified School District, 858 F.3d 1034, 1047–1051 (7th Cir. 2017); Dodds v. US Department of Education, 845 F.3d 217, 221 (6th Cir. 2016); Glenn v. Brumby, 663 F.3d 1312, 1316 (11th Cir. 2011); Smith v. City of Salem, 378 F.3d 566, 574 (6th Cir. 2004); Schwenk v. Hartford, 204 F.3d 1187, 1201–1203 (9th Cir. 2000); Macy v. Holder, No. 0120120821, 2012 WL 1435995, *7 (EEOC 20 April 2012). But see Etsitty v. Utah Transit Auth., 502 F.3d 1215, 1224 (10th Cir. 2007).

31 NALSA, supra note 29, at para. 59.

32 Schroer v. Billington, 577 F. Supp. 2d 293 (D.D.C. 2008).

33 P, supra note 29, at paras. 20–21.

the ECJ's opinion was quite short, it suggested that treating an individual unfavorably due the individual's sex reassignment is inherently sex discrimination.

The categorical rationale is yet another reason for understanding gender identity discrimination to be sex discrimination. This rationale recognizes the possibility of there being more than two sex categories. Some people have a gender identity that does not fit neatly within the male/female binary. A non-binary identity can be considered as a sex category beyond the traditional male/female categories. In this view, discriminating against someone for identifying with a non-binary sex category is sex discrimination. As the India Supreme Court explained: "The discrimination on the ground of 'sex' … includes discrimination on the ground of gender identity. The expression 'sex' used in Articles 15 and 16 [of the Constitution] is not just limited to biological sex of male or female, but intended to include people who consider themselves to be neither male or female."[34] To be sure, many transgender people consider themselves to be male or female, as opposed to identifying with a non-binary sex category. Nonetheless, as long as an employer perceives a transgender employee as belonging to a non-binary sex category and discriminates against the employee for that reason, such mistreatment would be considered sex discrimination according to the categorical rationale.

II.C *Objections*

There have been several objections to conceptualizing SOGI discrimination as forms of sex discrimination. The persuasiveness of these objections may depend on contextual factors that differ from one jurisdiction to another. The first objection is that broadening the conceptualization of sex discrimination to subsume SOGI discrimination violates the original meaning or purpose behind sex discrimination bans.[35] From a legal standpoint, the persuasiveness of this argument depends on the jurisdiction's existing framework for legal interpretation. For example, we can imagine being in a jurisdiction that bans sex discrimination through both constitutional and statutory provisions. Additionally, imagine that when those provisions were enacted, no one envisioned the sex discrimination bans being used to combat SOGI discrimination. Whether this jurisdiction should now regard SOGI discrimination as sex discrimination depends on the jurisdiction's approach to constitutional and statutory interpretation. If the jurisdiction adheres closely to originalism and deems legislative intent determinative, applying the sex discrimination

34 NALSA, supra note 29, at para. 59.

35 For examples of cases embracing this objection, see Smith, supra note 26; Ministry of Defence, ex parte Smith, supra note 26.

provision to SOGI claims may well be inappropriate.[36] However, in contexts like US employment discrimination law, in which the Supreme Court has stated that Title VII's coverage is not limited to "the principal evil Congress was concerned with when it enacted Title VII,"[37] interpreting sex discrimination provisions to cover SOGI claims is more fitting.[38]

Note that, even if SOGI claims were not contemplated when the government enacted its sex discrimination ban, doctrines of originalism and legislative intent do not necessarily preclude SOGI claims. Consider, for example, the possibility that sex discrimination legislation was clearly intended to combat discrimination based on sex stereotypes. The legislators may not have understood how sex stereotyping gives rise to SOGI discrimination and, therefore, may not have contemplated applying their law to SOGI discrimination. Yet, if the original intent of the legislation was to combat discrimination based on sex stereotypes, the anti-stereotyping principle should logically extend to plaintiffs in cases where sex stereotyping caused SOGI discrimination.[39]

The second objection to regarding SOGI discrimination as sex discrimination is what I will call the symmetry defense. Consider an employer who refuses to hire gay men and lesbians because he disapproves of homosexuality. The employer might argue that there is no sex discrimination because he equally disapproves of both male homosexuals and female homosexuals. Likewise, he may argue that he equally disapproves of both transgender men and transgender women. This hypothetical employer's claim is that symmetrical treatment of men and women renders his actions nondiscriminatory.[40]

There are two weaknesses to the symmetry defense. First is that discrimination that is formally symmetrical is still problematic from a normative perspective because it still reflects and reinforces gender stereotypes that sex

36 For background on "evolutionary versus fixed meaning" approaches to statutory interpretation and "originalist" versus "living" approaches to constitutional interpretation, see Kent Greenawalt, "Constitutional and Statutory Interpretation," in *Oxford Handbook of Jurisprudence and Philosophy of Law* (Jules L. Coleman, Kenneth Einar Himma, & Scott J. Shapiro eds.) (Oxford University Press 2004).

37 Oncale v. Sundowner Offshore Services, Inc., 523 U.S. 75, 79 (1998).

38 See Zarda, supra note 25; Hively, supra note 25.

39 For this volume's discussion about how sexual orientation discrimination relates to sex stereotyping, see Part II.A. For the discussion about how gender identity discrimination relates to sex stereotypes, see Part II.B.

40 For an example of a case embracing this objection, see Grant, supra note 25. For criticism of this argument, see, e.g., Nan D. Hunter, "The Sex Discrimination Argument in Gay Rights Cases," 9 *Journal of Law & Policy* 397, 401–403 (2001); Robert Wintemute, "Recognising New Kinds of Direct Sex Discrimination: Transsexualism, Sexual Orientation and Dress Codes," 60 *Modern Law Review* 334, 339–341 (1997).

discrimination law seeks to dismantle.[41] An employer who tells men that they must be stereotypically masculine by marrying a woman, and vice versa, entrenches gender stereotypes regardless of whether his heterosexual marriage requirement is symmetrically applied to both men and women. Second, his heterosexual marriage requirement may be formally symmetrical, but it is not symmetrical in its effects. Of course, the requirement has adverse effects on gays, lesbians, and bisexuals. In many cultural traditions, the reinforcement of sex stereotypes also has an adverse effect on women. As commentators such as Andrew Koppelmen, Sylvia Law, and Robert Wintemute among others have long acknowledged, the perpetuation of sex stereotypes reinforces patriarchal gender roles for men and women.[42]

A third objection to treating SOGI discrimination as sex discrimination is that it is morally insufficient. This framing reduces anti-LGBT bias to an issue of sexism and sexism alone, whereas a stronger moral message against anti-LGBT bias would be made if the government were to put SOGI front and center by declaring SOGI to be protected categories of their own. As Edward Stein put it, "when a law that discriminates on the basis of sexual orientation is overturned in the face of the sex discrimination argument, the central moral debates about homosexuality are bracketed."[43] Stein's observation could be expanded to critique the framing of gender identity claims as sex discrimination claims.

Note that this critique about moral insufficiency does not suggest that it is legally or logically incorrect to treat SOGI discrimination as sex discrimination. Rather, the critique suggests that winning cases against SOGI discrimination by relying on sex discrimination arguments fails to completely address

41 The Convention on the Elimination of Discrimination Against Women (CEDAW) calls for the elimination of "stereotyped roles for men and women." Convention on the Elimination of Discrimination Against Women (CEDAW) (1980), Art. 5. For a discussion on grounding LGBTI rights in CEDAW's anti-stereotyping principle, see Rikki Holtmaat & Paul Post, "Enhancing LGBTI Rights by Changing the Interpretation of the Convention on the Elimination of All Forms of Discrimination Against Women?," 33 *Nordic Journal of Human Rights* 319 (2005).

42 See Andrew Koppelman, "Why Discrimination Against Lesbians and Gay Men Is Sex Discrimination," 69 *NYU Law Review* 197 (1994); Law Sylvia A. Law, "Homosexuality and the Social Meaning of Gender," 1988 *Wisconsin Law Review* 187 (1988); Wintemute, supra note 40.

43 Edward Stein, "Evaluating the Sex Discrimination Argument for Gay and Lesbian Rights," 49 *UCLA Law Review* 471, 515 (2001). For variations on this argument, see Martha C. Nussbaum, *From Disgust to Humanity: Sexual Orientation and Constitutional Law*, at 115 (Oxford University Press 2010); John Gardner, "On the Ground of Her Sex(uality)," 18 *Oxford Journal of Legal Studies* 167, 182–183 (1998).

underlying evils. To address this insufficiency, it would be ideal for courts to recognize SOGI as protected categories of their own, while recognizing that sexual orientation discrimination and gender identity discrimination are also forms of sex discrimination. This was the approach taken by the district court in the much-publicized legal challenge against California's former ban on same-sex marriage.[44] Although the court did not address gender identity, the court did recognize that banning same-sex marriage amounted to both impermissible sexual orientation discrimination *and* impermissible sex discrimination. This approach expresses a strong moral message against heterosexism while also illuminating the overlap between heterosexism and sexism. In some contexts, however, courts may not have the legal authority to recognize sexual orientation and gender identity as protected categories of their own.[45] Thus, from a pragmatic perspective, it is sometimes necessary for advocates to rely solely on sex discrimination claims.[46]

III SOGI as Protected Categories of Their Own

Separate from the question of whether SOGI discrimination is a form of prohibited sex discrimination is the question of whether sexual orientation and gender identity are protected categories in and of themselves. Many jurisdictions around the world have answered this question in the affirmative.[47] Indeed, many more jurisdictions have chosen to recognize sexual orientation and gender identity as protected categories themselves, as opposed to protecting against SOGI discrimination through sex discrimination laws.

Jurisdictions have taken divergent paths to recognizing sexual orientation and gender identity as protected categories. Part III.A discusses the most straightforward path, which is to explicitly list sexual orientation and gender identity as protected categories in discrimination laws. Parts III.B and III.C examine an alternative path, whereby courts deem sexual orientation and gender identity to be protected categories through the exercise of judicial power.

44 Perry v. Schwarzenegger, 704 F. Supp. 2d 921 (N.D. Cal. 2010).

45 In the California case discussed above, the court was interpreting the US Constitution's open-ended Equal Protection Clause. This constitutional provision does not enumerate any protected categories. Thus, courts have needed to define constitutionally protected categories through case law. In the United States, the conventional wisdom is that courts do not have similar authority to add new protected categories to antidiscrimination statutes that already include an exhaustive list of protected categories.

46 See Zarda, supra note 25; Hively, supra note 25.

47 Illustrative examples will be discussed in Part III.A–B.

This usually happens in the context of constitutional adjudication and in the adjudication of international human rights. Part III.B sketches a picture of the legal landscape, showing that jurisdictions at various levels—international, regional, national, and subnational—have taken this judicial approach. Part III.C then illustrates the range of reasons that jurisdictions have offered for recognizing sexual orientation and gender identity as protected categories through judicial power.

Before embarking on this Part's analysis, a clarification is in order: for economy of language, this Part will often speak about jurisdictions collectively, referring to jurisdictions that, as a group, recognize sexual orientation and gender identity as protected categories. This does not mean that all of the individual jurisdictions within this aggregation recognize *both* sexual orientation *and* gender identity as protected categories. Some jurisdictions recognize only sexual orientation as a protected category.[48] Although it happens much more rarely, a jurisdiction may also recognize only gender identity but not sexual orientation.[49]

III.A *Explicit Protections*

Numerous jurisdictions around the world now have laws that explicitly recognize sexual orientation and gender identity as protected categories. The first area of relevant law is constitutional provisions concerning equality and discrimination. Note that the right to nondiscrimination may be framed as a right to equality. As Mpoki Mwakagali has explained, equality and nondiscrimination are two sides of the same coin.[50] According to a legal survey conducted by Raub et al. in 2014, ten national constitutions contained a right to equality based on sexual orientation,[51] and among those constitutions, five contained language specifically protecting the right to sexual orientation equality in the

48 For example, as discussed in Part III.A, ten countries have constitutions that explicitly ban sexual orientation discrimination, but only five of those ten also ban gender identity discrimination.

49 For example, India's Supreme Court has stated that gender identity is a protected category under constitutional law, but it has not declared that sexual orientation is a protected category as well. See NALSA, supra note 29.

50 Mwakagali, supra note 13, at 2.

51 The ten countries were Bolivia, Ecuador, Fiji, Malta, Mexico, New Zealand, Portugal, South Africa, Sweden, and the United Kingdom. Amy Raub et al., "Protections of Equal Rights across Sexual Orientation and Gender Identity: An Analysis of 193 National Constitutions," 28 *Yale Journal of Law & Feminism* 149, 157 (2016). Raub et. al did not include Kosovo, perhaps because of its disputed statehood. It is worth noting that the 2008 Constitution of Kosovo, Art. 24(2), also lists sexual orientation as a protected category.

context of employment.[52] Five national constitutions contained a general right to equality based on gender identity,[53] and three protected the right to gender identity equality specifically with respect to employment.[54] After Raub et al. published their survey, one other country, Nepal, adopted a new constitution that protects "sexual minorities" against discrimination.[55]

Looking at their data in relative terms, Raub et al. found that only five percent of national constitutions explicitly protected a right to equality based on sexual orientation.[56] Further, only three percent explicitly protected a right to equality based on gender identity.[57] In contrast, 84 percent of national constitutions contained a provision that explicitly protected the right to equality based on sex.[58] This disparity underscores the practical relevance of the question examined in the previous Part of this volume: does SOGI discrimination constitute a form of sex discrimination? Because so many constitutions explicitly ban sex discrimination but not SOGI discrimination, human rights defenders may find it useful to argue that SOGI discrimination is already banned by these constitutions' sex discrimination provisions.

Beyond constitutional law, a growing number of jurisdictions are also passing legislative protections that explicitly recognize sexual orientation and gender identity as protected grounds.[59] One survey of laws published in 2017 found that 72 countries have statewide employment discrimination legislation recognizing sexual orientation as a protected category.[60] Many jurisdictions have also undertaken legislative reforms to prohibit sexual orientation discrimination in additional contexts, such as education, housing, and the provision of

---

52 The five countries were Bolivia, Ecuador, New Zealand, Portugal, and the United Kingdom. Id. at 158.

53 The five countries were Bolivia, Ecuador, Fiji, Malta, and the United Kingdom. Id. at 157.

54 The three countries were Bolivia, Ecuador, and the United Kingdom. Id. at 157–58.

55 Nepal Constitution of 2015, Sec. 18(3).

56 Id. at 157.

57 Id.

58 Id.

59 This volume draws a distinction between constitutions, which are typically entrenched, versus ordinary legislation, which typically is not entrenched. The volume draws this analytical distinction because it is so widely adopted in legal systems around the world. However, some jurisdictions such as the United Kingdom do not maintain this strict distinction. For background reading on the United Kingdom's uncodified and unentrenched constitution, see Eric Barendt, *An Introduction to Constitutional Law*, at 26–34 (Oxford University Press 1998).

60 Aengus Carroll & Lucas Ramón Mendos, ILGA, *State-Sponsored Homophobia: A World Survey of Sexual Orientation Laws: Criminalisation, Protection and Recognition*, at 8 (12th ed. 2017).

goods and services.[61] A variety of jurisdictions have also enacted legislation that explicitly bans discrimination based on gender identity.[62] Legislative reforms that make sexual orientation and gender identity protected categories have been undertaken not only by national governments, but also by subnational governments ranging from states and cities within the United States to provinces and municipalities in the Philippines.[63]

III.B *Protection by Analogy: The Landscape*

When codified law does not explicitly list sexual orientation or gender identity as protected categories, courts and quasi-judicial bodies might interpret open-ended equality protections to prohibit SOGI discrimination nonetheless. In other words, courts interpret these protections to create a presumption against SOGI discrimination, similar to how the law presumes that discrimination based on other protected categories is unlawful.[64] To the best of my knowledge, there have been no published reports that survey all the jurisdictions where tribunals have concluded that sexual orientation and/or gender identity discrimination are protected categories even though codified law does not expressly state so. Based on a cursory scan of jurisdictions, however, one sees that this approach has been adopted by a diverse range of jurisdictions at multiple levels: international, regional, national, and subnational.

At the international level, for example, the United Nations Committee on Economic, Social, and Cultural Rights (CESCR) has explained in a General Comment that the International Covenant on Economic, Social, and Cultural Rights (ICESCR) prohibits discrimination based on sexual orientation and gender identity.[65] The ICESCR guarantees that the rights in the treaty shall "be exercised without discrimination of any kind as to race, colour, sex,

61 Id. at 54–60.

62 See Muntarbhorn, supra note 6 (noting Australia, Germany, Sweden, and Quezon City in the Philippines as examples of jurisdictions that have legislation banning discrimination based on gender identity). To the best of my knowledge, there has not been any published research that comprehensively surveys laws around the world that make gender identity a protected category.

63 See Movement Advancement Project, supra note 14 (illustrating that 22 states within the United States include sexual orientation, and sometimes gender identity, as legislatively protected categories); Eric Julian Manalastas, *Anti-Discrimination Ordinances*, pages.upd.edu.ph/ejmanalastas/policies-ordinances (last visited 4 April 2018) (listing 2 provinces and 11 municipalities in the Philippines that include sexual orientation and/or gender identity as protected categories).

64 Cf. Mwakagali, supra note 13, at 2.

65 Committee on Economic, Social and Cultural Rights (CESCR), General Comment No. 20, UN Doc. E/C.12/GC/20, 2 July 2009, para. 32.

language, religion, political or other opinion, national or social origin, property, birth or other status."[66] Neither sexual orientation nor gender identity is expressly mentioned in this list of protected categories, but the CESCR has concluded that both sexual orientation and gender identity are protected as "other status[es]" that fall within the treaty's purview.[67]

Similarly, at the regional level, the European Court of Human Rights and the Inter-American Court of Human Rights have both held that sexual orientation is a protected category under their respective treaties, even though it is not specifically enumerated as such.[68] The Inter-American Court of Human Rights has stated that gender identity is a protected category as well.[69] Meanwhile, apex domestic courts in places ranging from Canada[70] to Hong Kong[71] and Taiwan[72] have held that sexual orientation is a protected category under constitutional law, even though it is not explicitly mentioned in the constitution. Subnational tribunals have also reached this conclusion.[73]

Most of the examples to be discussed in this section concern sexual orientation because there are very few judicial opinions on whether gender identity is a protected category unto itself.[74] Not all courts that have been presented with the opportunity to recognize sexual orientation as a protected category have chosen to do so. For example, in 2013, the Singapore Supreme Court's Court of Appeal distinguished sexual orientation from other grounds of discrimination that are explicitly protected in Singapore's constitution.[75] The court did not treat sexual orientation as a protected category and, therefore, subjected Singapore's discriminatory sodomy law to a highly deferential form of judicial review. Likewise, in upholding the criminalization of same-sex sodomy, the apex courts in Botswana and Zimbabwe could have declared sexual orientation

66 International Covenant on Economic, Social and Cultural Rights (ICESCR), Art. 2, para. 2.

67 CESCR, supra note 65, para. 32.

68 See, e.g., Karner v. Austria ECtHR, No. 40016/98, 24 July 2003; Atala-Riffo & Daughters v. Chile, IACtHR (Judgment) 24 February 2012, para. 91; Aaron Baker, "Proportional, Not Strict, Scrutiny: Against a U.S. 'Suspect Classifications' Model Under Article 14 ECHR in the U.K.," 56 *American Journal of Comparative Law* 847, 888–889 (2008).

69 Atala-Riffo & Daughters, supra note 68, para. 91.

70 Vriend v. Alberta, [1998] 1 S.C.R. 493, 495.

71 Secretary for Justice v. Yau Yuk Lung Zigo, [2007] 10 HKCFAR 335.

72 Judicial Yuan (JY) Interpretation No. 748 (2017).

73 E.g., Varnum v. Brien, 763 N.W.2d 862 (Iowa 2009); Kerrigan v. Commissioner of Public Health, 957 A.2d 407 (Connecticut 2008); In re Marriage Cases, 183 P.3d 384 (California 2008).

74 For an exceptional example where gender identity is recognized as a protected category, see Atala-Riffo & Daughters, supra note 68, para. 91. See also CESCR, supra note 65, para. 32.

75 Lim Meng Suang v. Attorney-General [2015] 1 SLR 26 (CA 2014).

to be a protected category, but they chose not to.[76] In the United States, some states' apex courts have also rejected the idea that sexual orientation is a protected category.[77]

It is worth noting that the United States is exceptional in its treatment of protected categories under constitutional law. The US Constitution does not explicitly list any protected categories,[78] but the US Supreme Court has held that certain types of discrimination warrant more rigorous judicial review than others.[79] Most jurisdictions subject discrimination based on any protected category to the same rigorous proportionality analysis, while discrimination based on unprotected categories are either reviewed under highly deferential standards or categorically rejected. In contrast, the United States has created multiple tiers of judicial review for equal protection cases.[80] For example, race discrimination is subject to "strict scrutiny," sex discrimination is subject to "intermediate scrutiny," and most other forms of discrimination are subject to deferential "rational basis review."[81]

The US Supreme Court has been opaque about what level of review should be applied to sexual orientation discrimination.[82] Many commentators have suggested that the Supreme Court has subjected sexual orientation discrimination to a de facto tier of review that commentators call "rational basis review with bite," which is not as rigorous as that which the Court applies to race or sex discrimination, but is also not as deferential as traditional rational basis review. The Court itself has not used the phrase "rational basis review with bite."[83] Indeed, it has been unclear about whether, or to what extent, sexual orientation is a protected category, thus prompting criticism from commentators who have chided the Court for its opacity.[84] Meanwhile, the Court has yet to hear a constitutional case concerning gender identity discrimination.

---

76 EK Quansah makes this point in "Same-sex Relationships in Botswana: Current Perspectives and Future Prospects," 4 *African Human Rights Law Journal* 201 (2004).

77 E.g., Andersen v. King County, 138 P.3d 963, 974–975 (Washington 2006); Conaway v. Deane, 932 A.2d 571, 607–608 (Maryland 2007).

78 The US Constitution protects people's rights to "the equal protection of the laws," but it does not enumerate any specific protected categories. United States Constitution, Amendment XIV, Sec. 1.

79 See Holning Lau & Hillary Li, "American Equal Protection and Global Convergence," 86 *Fordham Law Review* 1251, 1266–1267 (2017).

80 See id.

81 See id.

82 See Hunter, supra note 14.

83 See Lau & Li, supra note 79, at 1269.

84 See id.; Peter Nicolas, "Obergefell's Squandered Potential," 6 *California Law Review Circuit* 137, 137–144 (2015).

III.C *Protection by Analogy: Underlying Reasoning*

SOGI discrimination has presented courts with a vexing question: if the constitution's equality clause does not explicitly say that a particular characteristic is protected, what should be the criteria for determining whether the characteristic qualifies as a prohibited ground of discrimination? In some jurisdictions, courts may face this question for the first time when reviewing cases concerning sexual orientation or gender identity discrimination. To answer whether these characteristics are protected categories, even though the constitution does not enumerate them as such, courts have generally reasoned by analogy.[85]

One approach to this analogical inquiry would be to say that SOGI discrimination is so similar to sex discrimination that sexual orientation and gender identity should themselves be protected statuses just like sex. The Delhi High Court in India adopted this reasoning to conclude that sexual orientation is a protected category.[86] The Court did not say that sexual orientation discrimination is a form of sex discrimination, as some other courts have;[87] it stated instead that "sexual orientation is a ground analogous to sex and that discrimination on the basis of sexual orientation is not permitted …"[88]

Most courts, however, have not relied on reasoning that analogizes SOGI to sex. Instead of analogizing only to sex, courts have sought to identify a set of factors for determining whether characteristics qualify as prohibited grounds of discrimination. The factors for protection have varied from jurisdiction to jurisdiction. Even within a single jurisdiction, the factors have sometimes evolved. Indeed, there is no consensus among courts and commentators on a test for determining whether a characteristic is protected. It is beyond the scope of this volume to propose any sort of model test. Instead, the remainder of this section provides background on some of the factors that have emerged, and been debated, in the jurisprudence. These factors include (1) whether there has been a history or frequentness of irrational discrimination based on the characteristic, (2) whether groups defined by the characteristic are politically powerless, and (3) whether the characteristic is immutable.

The first factor is a history or frequentness of unreasonable discrimination based on the particular characteristic. For example, the Supreme Court of Canada has said that analogous grounds of discrimination—i.e., grounds

85 Susanne Baer, "Equality," in *Oxford Handbook of Comparative Constitutional Law*, at 996–997 (András Sajó & Michel Rosenfeld eds.) (Oxford University Press 2012).

86 Pritam Baruah, "Logic and Coherence in *Naz Foundation*: The Arguments of Nondiscrimination, Privacy, and Dignity," 2 *NUJS Law Review* 515 (2009).

87 For examples of this this reasoning, see Part II.A.

88 Naz Foundation v. Government of NCT of Delhi, W.P. (C) No. 7455/2001, 160 (2009) DLT 277, para. 104.

that are not enumerated in the constitution but are sufficiently analogous—"often serve as the basis for stereotypical decisions made not on the basis of merit ..."[89] This observation was a core component to the court's conclusion that sexual orientation is a protected category even though the constitution does not explicitly say so.[90] More recently, in its landmark same-sex marriage case, the Taiwan Constitutional Court concluded that sexual orientation is a protected category after it took note of historical discrimination against gays and lesbians based on stereotypes.[91] Other jurisdictions have similarly looked to the history and frequentness of unreasonable discrimination as a factor for determining protected status.[92]

This rationale advances certain normative principles of equality law, such as anti-stereotyping and anti-subordination, both of which are connected to the protection of human dignity. If a characteristic has often been the basis for irrational discrimination—discrimination stemming from problematic stereotyping or subordination—courts have reason to double-check the political branches for recommitting these sins. Thus, the history or frequentness rationale justifies a presumption against such discrimination. Note, however, that determining protected categories based on the history or frequentness of discrimination may result in under-inclusiveness because new forms of irrational discrimination may arise. In such situations, courts should be empowered to scrutinize the discrimination if their aim is to combat irrational stereotyping and subordination.[93]

Political power is another factor that various courts around the world have invoked. This factor is often traced back to the US Supreme Court opinion in *United States v. Carolene Products Company*.[94] The Court suggested that,

89 Corbière v. Canada, [1999] 2 S.C.R. 203. In Corbière, the Supreme Court of Canada also noted that analogous grounds of discrimination are based on "a personal characteristic that is immutable or changeable only at unacceptable cost to personal identity." Id. at 206. This immutability requirement is discussed below in notes 103–110 and accompanying text.

90 Vriend, supra note 70.

91 JY Interpretation 748, supra note 72.

92 At the international level, consider the CESCR. It has stated that analogous grounds of discrimination "are commonly recognized when they reflect the experience of social groups that are vulnerable and have suffered and continue to suffer marginalization." CESCR, supra note 65, para. 27.

93 For example, imagine a hypothetical society that had not experienced racial discrimination until very recently because the society had been racially homogenous until the recent arrival of immigrants from a different racial background. One may argue that race should still be a protected category in this country despite its lack of prior race discrimination.

94 304 U.S. 144 (1938).

if a group of people defined by a particular characteristic has lacked political power, such political powerlessness supports making that group status a protected category. Specifically, the case referenced social groups that lack political power due to being "discrete and insular minorities" such as racial and religious minorities.[95] Commentators have explained protecting such disempowered groups in terms of democratic theory: because certain social groups are unable to advance their interests through democratic processes (e.g., due to the group's small size), courts have good reason to play a particularly large role in protecting such groups against prejudices held by the democratic majority.[96] In these cases, judicial review of discriminatory actions corrects for inadequacies in democratic governance. As the US Supreme Court explained, the political powerlessness rationale protects groups "in need of extraordinary protection from the majoritarian political process."[97]

The political powerlessness factor can work in conjunction with the history or frequentness factor. A social group may lack political power due to a history of stereotyping and subordination. For example, although women are not a numerical minority in most societies, they may be politically disadvantaged because of societal structures shaped by a history of sexist stereotypes and subordination. In this situation, granting women protected status addresses not only democratic failures, but also the history of sex-based stereotyping and subordination.

A variety of courts—ranging from courts in the United States to the Taiwan Constitutional Court—have pointed to the comparative political disadvantage of gays and lesbians as a factor that supports treating sexual orientation as a protected category.[98] Yet, the political powerlessness factor has its shortcomings. One line of criticism centers on the difficulty in operationalizing the factor. How exactly is political power to be determined?[99] If women and/or members of racial minority groups are elected to some of the country's highest political offices, does that fact suggest that their respective social groups are now politically powerful? Would it necessarily follow that those social groups

95 Id. at 152–153 n. 4.

96 See, e.g., Cass Sunstein, *The Partial Constitution*, at 143 (Harvard University Press 1993); John Hart Ely, *Democracy and Distrust*, at 153–170 (Harvard University Press 1980).

97 San Antonio Independent School District v. Rodriguez, 411 U.S. 1, 28 (1973).

98 E.g., Windsor v. United States, 699 F.3d 169, 182–185 (2nd Cir. 2012); JY Interpretation 748, supra note 72; Varnum, supra note 73, at 894–895.

99 For scholarship that grapples with the question of how to determine political power, see, e.g., Nicholas O. Stephanopoulos, "Political Powerlessness," 90 *NYU Law Review* 1527 (2015); Darren Lenard Hutchinson, "'Not Without Political Power': Gays and Lesbians, Equal Protection, and the Suspect Class Doctrine," 65 *Alabama Law Review* 975 (2013–2014).

are no longer protected categories? These are questions that have vexed commentators. In some jurisdictions, courts have refused to recognize sexual orientation as a protected category in part because they found gays and lesbians to have political power.[100] However, there is a normative critique that, even if it is abundantly clear that previously subordinated social groups now have political power (e.g., blacks in South Africa), the characteristics that define those social groups (e.g., race) should still be a protected category because discrimination based on that category is rarely rational. In this sense, making political powerlessness a requirement for protected categories creates an underinclusive list of protected categories.

Indeed, in some jurisdictions, the relevance of political powerlessness to judicial reasoning seems to be in decline although court opinions have not made clear why that is so. For example, in the United States, despite *Carolene Products* having inspired theories about political powerlessness, the Supreme Court has gone on to treat race and sex as protected (i.e., "suspect" and "quasi-suspect") categories even when it was whites or men—politically powerful groups—who complained of discrimination.[101] In Canada, the Supreme Court had mentioned political power as a factor in identifying analogous grounds of constitutional protection in the past, but more recent articulations of the criteria for protected status have omitted any reference to political power.[102]

Immutability is another factor that is sometimes considered by courts when determining whether a category is protected. Courts initially defined immutability narrowly as biological characteristics that cannot be changed. For example, the US Supreme Court referred to race and sex as "immutable" because, according to the Court, these biological traits are "accidents of birth" that cannot be changed.[103] This conceptualization of immutability is tied to the notion that people should not be discriminated against based on traits that they cannot control.[104] However, if a trait can be modified, individuals bear more responsibility for protecting themselves by conforming to the government's

---

100 See, e.g., Andersen, supra note 77; Conaway, supra note 77.

101 See Julie A. Nice, "Equal Protection's Antinomies and the Promise of a Co-Constitutive Approach," 85 *Cornell Law Review* 1392, 1400–1402 (2000).

102 For a discussion on the evolution of relevant cases in Canada, see Rosalind Dixon, "The Supreme Court of Canada and Constitutional (Equality) Baselines," 50 *Osgoode Hall Law Journal* 637 (2003).

103 Frontiero v. Richardson, 411 U.S. 677, 678–679 (1973) (plurality opinion). Notwithstanding the US Supreme Court's understanding of race and sex being immutable, whether one's race and sex can be changed remains contested. Note, for example, that a growing number of jurisdictions allow transgender individuals to change their sex on government identification documents.

104 Id. at 678–679.

demands. Thus, laws that discriminate based on immutable characteristics ought to be subject to strong judicial review.

This traditional conceptualization of immutability has been criticized for being too narrow,[105] and courts have begun to take a more expansive view. The traditional immutability requirement could not explain, for example, why non-biological traits such as religion are so commonly considered protected categories. Courts have now broadened the definition of immutability to include traits that can only be changed with great difficulty or at great cost to an individual's sense of self.[106] Some commentators have referred to this as "soft"[107] or "constructive"[108] immutability. Certain jurisdictions no longer even use the word "immutability" to describe soft immutability, but they arrive at the same outcome through different language. For example, the Supreme Court of Canada has said that protected analogous categories are usually "immutable *or changeable only at unacceptable cost to personal identity*."[109] Relatedly, in Hong Kong, the Court of Final Appeal has stated that protected categories implicate "core-values relating to personal or human characteristics" including sexual orientation.[110] Although the court did not use the term "immutability," its reference to "personal or human characteristics" comports with the notion of soft immutability encompassing traits that can only be changed at great cost to personal identity.

This move from traditional immutability to soft immutability has made it more likely that courts will treat sexual orientation and gender identity as protected categories. Although the biological basis of sexual orientation and gender identity are contested, it seems less controversial to say that these are deeply personal characteristics—ones that can only be changed at great cost to the individual.[111]

105 For a discussion of such criticisms, see Jessica A. Clarke, "Against Immutability," 125 *Yale Law Journal* 2, 18–23 (2015).

106 For a discussion of this broadened conception of immutability in Canada, see Dixon, supra note 102, at 648–652. For a discussion of cases from the United States, see Clarke, supra note 105, at 21–27.

107 E.g. Edward Stein, "Immutability and Innateness Arguments About Lesbian, Gay, and Bisexual Rights," 89 *Chicago-Kent Law Review* 597 (2014); Joseph Landau, "'Soft Immutability' and 'Imputed Gay Identity': Recent Developments in Transgender and Sexual-Orientation-Based Asylum Law," 32 *Fordham Urban Law Journal* 237 (2005).

108 E.g., Dixon, supra note 102.

109 Corbière, supra note 89, at 206 (emphasis added).

110 Fok Chun Wa v. Hospital Authority, [2012] 15 H.K.C.F.A.R. 409 para. 5 (C.F.A.).

111 See Stein, supra note 107, at 634.

IV Sequential Development of SOGI Discrimination Protections

As SOGI discrimination protections have developed around the world, so have narratives about the trajectories for incrementally developing these protections. This Part describes and interrogates two primary narratives. The first narrative states that rights protections proceed in a particular order based on the type of protection. It claims that sexual orientation nondiscrimination is first protected with respect to the regulation of sexual activity, then employment, then same-sex partnership recognition through alternatives to marriage, then equal marriage rights, then parenting rights. The narrative also suggests that rights to gender identity nondiscrimination typically lags behind sexual orientation nondiscrimination. A second narrative concerns cultural groups. This narrative suggests that Western states lead in the development of SOGI nondiscrimination protections and then the rest of the world follows. This part of the volume interrogates these conventional narratives about trajectories of change and reveals their flaws. It will also consider the potential harms of perpetuating these flawed narratives.

IV.A *Rethinking Sequential Rights*

Commentators have observed that the development of LGBT rights often follows familiar sequences, especially with respect to discrimination based on sexual orientation. Kees Waaldijk, for example, observed that European countries tended to follow a similar path: first a country would decriminalize sodomy, then equalize age-of-consent laws for same-sex and different-sex sexual activity, then pass national antidiscrimination legislation pertaining to sexual orientation, then offer same-sex couples some form of legal recognition short of marriage, followed by full marriage equality.[112] Drawing on the research of Waaldijk, scholars such as William Eskridge and Yuval Merin wrote that a similar pattern might be expected in the United States.[113] In my own conversations in various parts of the world, I have heard some advocates adhere to

112 Kees Waaldijk, "Civil Developments: Patterns of Reform in the Legal Position of Same-Sex Partners in Europe," 17 *Canadian Journal of Family Law* 62 (2000); Kees Waaldijk, "Others May Follow: The Introduction of Marriage Quasi-Marriage, and Semi-Marriage for Same-Sex Couples in European Countries," 38 *New England Law Review* 569 (2003) [hereinafter "Others May Follow"]; Kees Waaldijk, "Standard Sequences in the Legal Recognition of Homosexuality—Europe's Past, Present, and Future," 4 *Australian Gay & Lesbian Law Journal* 50 (1994) [hereinafter "Standard Sequences"].

113 William N. Eskridge Jr., "Comparative Law and the Same-Sex Marriage Debate: A Step-by-Step Approach Toward State Recognition," 31 *McGeorge Law Review* 641, 647–648 (1999–2000); Yuval Merin, *Equality for Same-Sex Couples: The Legal Recognition of Gay Partnerships in Europe and the United States*, at 326 (University of Chicago Press 2012).

the received wisdom that law reform must follow in a particular sequence of steps that reflects the European experience.

In the time since Waaldijk's research, however, non-European jurisdictions have deviated from this sequence of rights development. Consider, for example, the United States. The United States has differed from Europe in several ways. In contrast to the European experience, the United States extended nationwide marriage rights to same-sex couples before protecting LGB persons from discrimination in contexts such as private employment, housing, and public accommodations. One explanation for this is the relatively strong role played by courts in the United States. When Waaldijk studied Europe, the countries that had legalized same-sex marriage had done so through legislative means.[114] In the United States, however, courts have played a large role in the legalization of same-sex marriage. At the national level, the Supreme Court ruled in *Obergefell v. United States* that state bans on same-sex marriage are unconstitutional, which in effect brought same-sex marriage to the entire country.[115] By the time the Supreme Court decided *Obergefell*, same-sex marriage was already legal in thirty-seven states and the District of Columbia.[116]

Notably, when the US Supreme Court decided *Obergefell* in 2015, the United States lacked—and it still lacks—a federal law banning SOGI discrimination in areas such as private employment, housing, and public accommodations. Due to the doctrine of "state action," US courts lack power to address discrimination in these contexts through constitutional law.[117] Meanwhile, Congress has refused to pass legislation explicitly banning SOGI discrimination in the private sphere despite the efforts of civil rights advocates.[118] At the time of this writing, nearly three years after *Obergefell* was decided, a majority of states within the United States still lack any state-level protections against discrimination based on sexual orientation or gender identity in the context of private-sector employment, housing, and public accommodation.[119]

As discussed above, some federal courts of appeal in the United States now interpret Title VII's ban on sex-based employment discrimination to subsume

114 E.g., Waaldijk, "Others May Follow," supra note 112 (discussing legislative acts that legalized same-sex marriage in the Netherlands and in Belgium).

115 See Obergefell v. Hodges, 135 S. Ct. 2584 (2015).

116 See Holning Lau, "Comparative Perspectives on Strategic Remedial Delays," 91 *Tulane Law Review* 259, 270–271 (2016).

117 See United States v. Morrison, 529 U.S. 598, 621 (2000); The Civil Rights Cases, 109 U.S. 3, 10–11 (1883). See also Erwin Chemerinsky, *Constitutional Law: Principles and Policies*, at Sec. 6.4 (Wolters Kluwer, 5th ed. 2015).

118 See Keith Cunningham-Parmeter, "Marriage Equality, Workplace Inequality: The Next Gay Rights Battle," 67 *Florida Law Review* 1099, 1144–1145 (2016).

119 See Movement Advancement Project, supra note 14.

sexual orientation discrimination.[120] Note, however, that these courts did not adopt this position until after *Obergefell*.[121] In reaching their decisions, the federal appellate courts in the Second and Seventh Circuits both cited *Obergefell*; they noted how paradoxical it would be to protect an individual's right to marry someone of the same sex but then fail to protect that individual against being fired from work for entering a same-sex marriage.[122] Marriage equality in the United States thus contributed to the eventual development of employment discrimination rights via case law.

In this sense, the United States presents a very different narrative from that of Europe. In much of Europe, the prohibition of sexual orientation discrimination through legislation, including European Union law, influenced social norms in ways that facilitated the development of partnership recognition legislation and the eventual legalization of same-sex marriage.[123] This pattern held true for some states in the United States, especially those that legalized same-sex marriage through legislation or referendum.[124] However, in most parts of the United States, and at the federal level, legalization of same-sex marriage was achieved through litigation that predated development of other antidiscrimination protections.[125]

While I have been focusing on the United States as a contrasting case to Europe, the United States is not alone. On the other side of the world is the example of Hong Kong. Like in the United States, courts in Hong Kong have played a pivotal role in advancing LGBT rights through constitutional law.[126] Indeed, Hong Kong's courts appear poised to extend legal recognition to same-sex couples under certain circumstances, even though Hong Kong's Legislative Council has yet to pass any legislation to ban sexual orientation

120 See supra note 25 and accompanying text.

121 See Zarda, supra note 25; Hively, supra note 25.

122 See Zarda, supra note 25, at 131 n.33; Hively, supra note 25, at 342, 349–350.

123 See Merin, supra note 113, at 314–318, 326–333.

124 These states include Connecticut, Delaware, Hawaii, Illinois, Maine, Maryland, Minnesota, New Hampshire, New York, Rhode Island, Vermont, and Washington. The District of Columbia also followed this pattern.

125 See National Conference of State Legislatures, *Same-Sex Marriage Laws*, 26 June 2015, www.ncsl.org/research/human-services/same-sex-marriage-laws.aspx (providing a history of the development of same-sex marriage rights in the United States); Jerome Hunt, *A State-by-State Examination of Nondiscrimination Laws and Policies* (Center for American Progress 2012) (providing a history of state-level SOGI discrimination bans in the United States).

126 See Yau Yuk Lung Zigo, supra note 71; Leung T.C. William Roy v. Secretary for Justice, [2006] 4 HKLRD 211 (CA); W v. Registrar of Marriages, [2013] 16 HKCFAR 112 (CFA); QT v. Director of Immigration, [2017] HKEC 2051 (CA). But see Leung Chun Kwong v. Secretary for the Civil Service, [2018] HKCA 318 (CA).

discrimination. In a case currently pending before Hong Kong's Court of Final Appeal, the court below held that, for immigration purposes, Hong Kong must recognize the union of two women who entered a civil partnership abroad.[127] The court ruled that doing otherwise would violate nondiscrimination protections in Hong Kong's Basic Law and Bill of Rights. There is also pending litigation concerning whether a same-sex couple that married overseas has a right to be recognized as married for civil servant spousal benefits and taxation purposes. Although the Court of First Instance ruled in favor of the same-sex couple with respect to civil servant benefits,[128] the Court of Appeal ruled against the couple.[129] The case is now likely to go to Hong Kong's Court of Final Appeal. While these cases are still pending, there is a good chance that Hong Kong's judiciary will ultimately recognize legal rights of same-sex couples, at least for certain purposes, to maintain fidelity to its compelling case law on sexual orientation discrimination.[130]

Although Hong Kong's courts have ruled that sexual orientation is a prohibited ground of discrimination under constitutional law,[131] those constitutional provisions do not regulate private contexts. Meanwhile, Hong Kong's government has declined to ban sexual orientation discrimination in private domains through legislation.[132] Because Hong Kong's law reform has been led by courts applying constitutional rights, Hong Kong seems poised to remedy discrimination with respect to the government's recognition of same-sex couples before addressing discrimination in contexts such as private employment. This sequence stands in contrast to the sequence from Europe.

Thus far, we have been discussing divergence from the European sequence regarding marriage and antidiscrimination legislation. There are additional points of divergence related to family law. In the United States, same-sex parenting rights often pre-dated partnership recognition rights, while the opposite was true for Europe.[133] It is not immediately clear why the United States did not follow the European sequence. One can speculate that the deviation

127 QT, supra note 126.

128 Leung Chun Kwong v. Secretary for the Civil Service, [2017] 2 HKLRD 1132 (CFI).

129 Leung Chun Kwong, supra note 126.

130 See supra note 126.

131 E.g., Yau Yuk Lung Zigo, supra note 71; Leung T.C. William Roy, supra note 126.

132 For a critique of the Legislative Council's failure to act, see Carole J. Petersen, "Sexual Orientation and Gender Identity in Hong Kong: A Case for the Strategic Use of Human Rights Treaties and the International Reporting Process," 14 *Asian-Pacific Law & Policy Journal* 28, 57–70 (2013).

133 See Merin, supra note 113, at 263; Nancy D. Polikoff, "Recognizing Partners but Not Parents/ Recognizing Parents but Not Partners: Gay and Lesbian Family Law in Europe and the United States," 17 *New York Law School Journal of Human Rights* 711 (2000).

was linked, in part, to patterns of family law reform driven by different-sex couples. For example, Douglas NeJaime has written about how gay and lesbian parents in the United States leveraged changing conceptions of parenthood spurred by different-sex couples' advocacy for rights related to assisted reproductive technologies and stepparent adoptions.[134] Europe did not experience a similar wave of law reform concerning different-sex couples' parenting rights. Nancy Polikoff has pointed out that there has been a greater need for adoptive parents in the United States compared with Europe, especially with respect to the number of children in the foster care system.[135] This backdrop is not specific to same-sex couples, but it helped same-sex couples when they volunteered to adopt children who needed homes. Polikoff also pointed to the larger role played by US courts in developing parenting rights.[136] These various factors may explain why same-sex couples in the United States were able to secure parenting rights before gaining legal recognition of their partnerships.

Another difference between Europe and the United States is the fact that European governments have typically extended non-marital forms of legal recognition to same-sex couples—such as rights to registered partnerships or recognition through de facto cohabitation—prior to extending full marriage rights to same-sex couples.[137] These "marriage light" alternatives to marriage were viewed by scholars as important stepping stones toward the legalization of same-sex marriage.[138] Most states in the United States, however, bypassed these stepping stones in legalizing same-sex marriage.[139] Many European jurisdictions first extended marriage alternatives to *different-sex* partnerships, for example through recognition of unregistered cohabitants.[140] Thus, there was already a precedent on which same-sex couples could rely to argue for similar partnership recognition.[141] In the United States, however, different-sex couples' options for legal recognition have tended to be limited to marriage and, where alternatives for different-sex couples do exist, they were

134 Douglas NeJaime, "Marriage Equality and the New Parenthood," 129 *Harvard Law Review* 1185, 1208–1212 (2016).

135 Polikoff, supra note 133, at 714.

136 Id.

137 See Waaldijk, "Others May Follow," supra note 112, at 589.

138 E.g., id.; Merin, supra note 113, at 314–318, 326–333.

139 For a discussion of civil unions, domestic partnerships, and other alternatives to marriage in the United States, see National Center for Lesbian Rights, *Marriage, Domestic Partnerships, and Civil Unions: Same-Sex Couples Within the United States* (2017).

140 See Waaldijk, "Standard Sequences," supra note 112, at 66.

141 Cf. Polikoff, supra note 133, at 714 (discussing European jurisdictions' interest in developing partnership recognition rights because of their social welfare systems).

usually created at the same time that marriage alternatives were created for same-sex couples.[142]

Yet another divergence worth noting relates to transgender rights. In the United States, the conventional narrative is that mainstream LGBT rights organizations focused, for a long time, on advancing sexual orientation rights, leaving gender identity issues on the back burner.[143] As a result, law reform regarding sexual orientation discrimination advanced more quickly. This is evident, for example, in the fact that the US Supreme Court has yet to hear a case about transgender discrimination. However, it has decided numerous sexual orientation rights cases, including cases in which gay and lesbian plaintiffs won landmark victories. The disparity of protection is also evident in the fact that most states with state-level SOGI antidiscrimination legislation first addressed sexual orientation before extending protections to gender identity.[144] At the time of this writing, two states—Wisconsin and New Hampshire—still only bar sexual orientation discrimination, but not gender identity discrimination.[145]

This narrative that places progress on sexual orientation rights before gender identity rights is not universal. There are jurisdictions outside the West that formalized protection of gender identity rights before protecting sexual orientation rights. For example, India and Pakistan have taken steps to address gender identity discrimination, yet these countries still criminalize same-sex sexual intimacy.[146] In fact, in 2014 the Supreme Court of India rejected a constitutional challenge to India's criminalization of homosexual sexual activity;[147] that same year, the Court handed down a sweeping ruling that the Indian constitution prohibits discrimination based on gender identity, and that individuals have a constitutional right to determine for themselves whether to identify as male, female, or a third gender.[148] In 2017, the Indian Supreme Court cast doubt on its earlier decision that upheld India's ban on same-sex intimacy,

142 See Erez Aloni, "Registering Relationships," 87 *Tulane Law Review* 573, 586–594 (2013).

143 See Minter, supra note 10.

144 See Hunt, supra note 125, at 3.

145 Movement Advancement Project, supra note 14.

146 See NALSA, supra note 29; Asad Hashim, "Pakistan passes landmark transgender rights law," *AlJazeera*, 9 May 2018, www.aljazeera.com/news/2018/05/pakistan-passes-landmark-transgender-rights-law-180509095207950.html. But see Dhrubo Jyoti, "Cut the Red Tape: Why the New Transgender Rights Bill Might Harm the Community," *Hindustan Times*, 26 July 2017 (highlighting delays in implementation of India's landmark NALSA decision).

147 Suresh Kumar Koushal v. Naz Foundation, SCC 1 (2014).

148 NALSA, supra note 29.

and it appears positioned to officially overrule that decision in the near future.[149] Still, my point here is that the Court's protection against gender identity discrimination preceded any future decriminalization of same-sex sexual intimacy. One potential reason for this is local culture, which has a long history of conceptualizing gender beyond two rigid categories. As the Indian Supreme Court noted: "Historical background of Transgenders in India ... [is such] that they were once treated with great respect, at least in the past, though not in the present."[150]

In sum, we should be cautious about viewing any specific sequencing of rights developments to be universal and natural. Developments in many parts of the world have not conformed to scholars' earlier observations about sequential ordering of rights developments in Europe. While further research is needed to determine more firmly the range of factors that contribute to the sequencing of rights development, this volume has illuminated three potential factors: the role of judicial review in the particular jurisdiction, the backdrop of law reform concerning issues not specific to SOGI (e.g., debates about artificial reproductive assistance), and local cultural history.

IV.B *Rethinking Westernization Narratives*

Another familiar narrative suggests that protections against SOGI discrimination originate in the West, and then the rest of the world imports these legal constructs belatedly. Indeed, writers sometimes describe the development of SOGI discrimination protections outside the West as a form of "westernization."[151] Such westernization narratives, however, are problematic for a few reasons that this section will explore.

First, westernization narratives are only accurate if one evaluates SOGI rights through a very particular lens. To be sure, by some important measures, the so-called West[152] does lead in developing protections against SOGI

149 In the landmark privacy case of Justice Puttaswamy (Ret'd) & Anr. v. Union of India and Ors., Writ Petition (Civil) No. 494 of 2012 (2017), the lead judgment and Justice Kaul's concurring judgment repudiated the *Koushal* case concerning same-sex sodomy, but they stopped short of officially overruling *Koushal* because a pending case is directly reevaluating *Koushal*. See also Menaka Guruswamy, "Justice K.S. Puttaswamy (Ret'd) and Anr v. Union of India and Ors," 111 *American Journal of International Law* 994 (2017).

150 NALSA, supra note 29, at para. 44.

151 I have previously critiqued this practice in Holning Lau, "The Language of Westernization in Legal Commentary," 61 *American Journal of Comparative Law* 507, 519–522 (2013).

152 The boundaries of "the West" are contested and some commentators have criticized the use of the term. See, e.g., Hugh Gusterson, "The Seven Deadly Sins of Samuel Huntington," in *Why America's Top Pundits Are Wrong*, at 28–29 (Catherine Besteman & Hugh Gusterson eds.) (University of California Press 2005).

discrimination. For example, most countries that have extended marriage rights to same-sex couples are part of the Western world. Painting with such broad brushstrokes, however, obscures significant deviations from the westernization narrative. Consider, for example, the abolition of discriminatory sodomy laws. At this particular point in history, it is true the countries that still criminalize sodomy are typically outside the Western world.[153] However, the history of sodomy laws does not fit a neat unidirectional narrative about the West leading the way.

The United States is understood to be a paradigmatic component of the West. Yet, when the US Supreme Court finally struck down discriminatory sodomy laws in the 2003 case of *Lawrence v. Texas*, it was not at the vanguard of change.[154] We can compare the United States with Asia. Twenty years prior to the *Lawrence* decision, Hong Kong's government conducted a study of sodomy laws in Asia and found that "more countries in the region tolerate consensual homosexual conduct by adults in private than penalize it, and that characteristically their legal systems only intervene where the homosexual activity involves some additional element of force, abuse of the young, oppression, fraud, absence of consent, exploitation or occurrence in public."[155] Indeed, by the time *Lawrence* was decided, many Asian jurisdictions had already decriminalized sodomy—or had never criminalized it in the first place.[156] In addition to obscuring this fact about decriminalization, narratives about Western progressiveness obscure the fact that it was typically Western colonial governments that established the discriminatory sodomy laws in Asia, and elsewhere, that local human rights defenders later sought to repeal.[157]

The case of sodomy laws is only one of several illustrations of the westernization narrative's flaws. Employment discrimination protections is another area in which the United States lags behinds many non-Western states. To date, the United States lacks nationwide protections against employment discrimination based on sexual orientation or gender identity.[158] Meanwhile, a non-negligible number of non-Western states have enacted such protections

153 See Carroll & Mendos, supra note 60, at 37–39.

154 See Lawrence v. Texas, 539 U.S. 558 (2003).

155 Law Reform Commission of Hong Kong, *Laws Governing Homosexual Conduct* (*Topic 2*), at 67–68 (1983), available at www.hkreform.gov.hk/en/publications/rhomosexual.htm.

156 See Holning Lau, "Grounding Conversations on Sexuality and Asian Law," 44 *U.C. Davis Law Review* 773, 776–778 (2011).

157 See, e.g., Douglas E. Sanders, "377 and the Unnatural Afterlife of British Colonialism in Asia," 4 *Asian Journal of Comparative Law* 1 (2009); Human Rights Watch, *This Alien Legacy: The Origins of "Sodomy" Laws in British Colonialism* (2008).

158 See discussion in supra notes 118–119 and accompanying text.

against sexual orientation discrimination and sometimes gender identity discrimination as well.[159]

Another challenge to the westernization narrative concerns constitutional protection against discrimination based on non-binary gender identities. The apex courts of Nepal, Pakistan, and India were early leaders in interpreting their constitutions to protect persons with non-binary gender identities.[160] Meanwhile, on the issue of marriage, we can contrast the European Court of Human Rights (ECtHR) with the Inter-American Court of Human Rights (IACtHR), whose jurisdiction mostly covers Latin America.[161] The ECtHR has held that the European Convention on Human Rights does not require member states to extend marriage rights to same-sex couples.[162] In contrast, the IACtHR based in Costa Rica has leaped ahead, holding that the Inter-American Convention on Human Rights requires states to grant marriage rights to same-sex couples.[163] Likewise, the IACtHR has stated that individuals have the right to be legally recognized in their gender identity based on self-determination,[164] whereas the ECtHR has allowed more onerous restrictions on the right to gender recognition.[165]

---

159 See Carroll & Mendos, note 60, at 46–59. To be sure, Western jurisdictions as a whole have a higher rate of establishing such protections, but this generalization obscures details worth noting.

160 On Nepal, see 2 *NJA Law Journal* 261 (2008) (translating Pant et al. v. Nepal, Writ No. 917, 21 December 2007). On India, see NALSA, supra note 29. On Pakistan, see Sean Dickson & Steve Sanders, "India, Nepal, and Pakistan: A Unique South Asian Constitutional Discourse on Sexual Orientation and Gender Identity," in *Social Difference and Constitutionalism in Pan-Asia*, at 340–344 (Susan H. Williams ed.) (Cambridge University Press 2013).

161 Many commentators do not consider Latin America to be a part of the so-called "West." See, e.g., Samuel P. Huntington, *The Clash of Civilizations and the Remaking of World Order* (Simon & Schuster 2011). Accordingly, recent developments in Latin America challenge assumptions that the Western world is always more advanced in protecting SOGI rights. Narratives about the development of SOGI rights are sometimes framed in terms of the Global North versus the Global South, with the assumption that SOGI rights travel from the former to the latter. Developments in Latin America challenge this assumption as well. See Katherine Brown & Catherine J. Nash, "Resisting LGBT Rights Where 'We Have Won': Canada and Great Britain," 13 *Journal of Human Rights* 322 (2014).

162 Chapin & Charpentier v. France, ECtHR, No. 40183/07, 9 June 2016; Schalk and Kopf v. Austria, ECtHR, No. 30141/04, 24 June 2010.

163 Advisory Opinion No. 24/17, IACtHR, 24 November 2017.

164 Id. at paras. 85–171.

165 See A.P., Garçon & Nicot v. France, ECtHR, Nos. 79885/12, 52471/13, 52596/13, 6 March 2017; Parry v. United Kingdom, ECtHR, No. 42971/05, 28 November 2016. See also Holning Lau, "Gender Recognition as Human Right," in *New Human Rights: Recognition, Novelty, Rhetoric* (Andreas von Arnauld, Kerstin Odendahl & Mart Susi eds., forthcoming 2018), available at ssrn.com/abstract=3056110.

Perpetuating flawed westernization narratives risks corrupting debates about law reform. For example, relying on the westernization narrative, opponents of SOGI rights sometimes claim that non-Western parts of the world ought to reject SOGI rights to rebuke the West.[166] Yet, these claims are problematic because SOGI rights transcend ties to the Western world. Non-Western parts of the world have drawn inspiration from a variety of sources, including indigenous ones, to support SOGI rights.[167] Indeed, as discussed earlier, non-Western jurisdictions have sometimes been more protective of SOGI rights than their Western counterparts.

Westernization narratives also undermine exchanges in the global marketplace of ideas by obscuring the fact that Western jurisdictions can learn from non-Western jurisdictions that have been leaders in protecting against SOGI discrimination. Various non-Western jurisdictions have been sites of knowledge production related to SOGI rights and should be acknowledged as such. Scholars, including myself, have argued to Western audiences that courts outside of the West are generating perspectives that ought to be studied by other jurisdictions around the world.[168] Sonia Katyal, for example, has argued that the Delhi High Court's opinion striking down India's sodomy law deserves attention because it is more forward-looking than the United States' decision in *Lawrence*.[169] She noted that "The Delhi High Court's *Naz Foundation* decision, although relying in part on *Lawrence* and other cases from the West, also transcended these decisions by relying on a wider host of non-Western jurisdictions ..."[170] Moreover, the *Naz Foundation* decision "transcended *Lawrence* in powerful and lasting ways ... reformed *Lawrence* by demonstrating its limitations."[171] Although a panel of the Indian Supreme Court eventually reversed the Delhi High Court in 2013,[172] the Supreme Court has agreed to revisit its decision and seems positioned to vindicate the Delhi High Court's earlier outcome.[173]

---

166 For acknowledgements and critiques of this claim, see e.g., Human Rights Watch, supra note 157; Lau, supra note 151, at 532–533; McGill, supra note 10, at 26–28; Stewart Chang, "Legacies of Exceptionalism and the Future of Gay Rights in Singapore," 46 *Hong Kong Law Journal* 72, 80 (2016).

167 See Lau, supra note 151, at 519–527.

168 See, e.g., Sonia Katyal, "The Dissident Citizen," 57 *UCLA Law Review* 1415 (2010); Holning Lau, "Marriage Equality and Family Diversity: Comparative Perspectives from the United States and South Africa," 85 *Fordham Law Review* 2615 (2017).

169 Katyal, supra note 168, at 1457–1458.

170 Id. at 1457.

171 Id. at 1458.

172 See Koushal, supra note 147.

173 See supra note 149.

Beyond the topic of sodomy, discussions about other issues similarly benefit from moving beyond a westernization narrative. Jurists around the world should study South Africa's case of *Minister of Home Affairs v. Fourie*, which made South Africa's constitutional court the first national apex court in the world to hold that excluding same-sex couples from marriage is a constitutional violation.[174] In previous writing, I have argued that *Fourie* ought not to be shadowed by *Obergefell v. Hodges* from United States because *Fourie* contains insights missing from the United States' decision. On gender identity, governments around the world might look to Argentina, which blazed a trail when it became the first country in the world to allow transgender individuals to obtain new identity documents reflecting their gender identity without imposing any medical requirements.[175] The Inter-American Commission of Human Rights later described Argentina's approach as a best practice for advancing goals of nondiscrimination.[176] Yet another example of non-Western jurisdictions being at the vanguard is the protection of persons with non-binary gender identities. As previously mentioned, the apex courts of Nepal, Pakistan, and India have all recognized and protected individuals who identify outside the male/female binary.[177] At the very least, these jurisdictions unsettle assumptions that Western courts may have about the binary nature of sex and gender categories.[178] In sum, certain parts of the non-Western world are advancing SOGI discrimination law in ways that warrant attention and careful study. Yet the overly simplistic narrative of westernization relegates these developments to the shadows.

V Drawbacks of SOGI Discrimination Protections

SOGI discrimination protections have prompted criticism, not only from social conservatives but also from progressive commentators who believe anti-discrimination frameworks are too constraining. Because the critiques from social conservatives are likely already familiar to readers, this volume focuses

---

174 Minister of Home Affairs v. Fourie, 2006 (1) SA 524 (CC).

175 Gender Identity Act, No. 26,743 of 23 May 2012 (Argentina). See also Emily Schmall, "Transgender Advocates Applaud New Law in Argentina: Far-Reaching Measure Is One of World's Most Liberal on Changing Sex," *International Herald Tribune*, 26 May 26 2012, at 6.

176 Inter-American Commission on Human Rights (IACommHR), *Violence Against LGBTI Persons*, at 222 (2015).

177 See supra note 160 and accompanying text.

178 See Holning Lau, "Law, Sexuality, and Transnational Perspectives," 5 *Drexel Law Review* 479, 485–486 (2013). Cf. also Dickson & Sanders, supra note 160, at 347 ("the decisions from India, Nepal, and Pakistan are fascinating decisions that rightfully occupy a prominent place in the broader global movement for SOGI rights.").

instead on examining two critiques from commentators who are sympathetic to expanding SOGI rights but are wary of working within an antidiscrimination framework. The first criticism is that the SOGI antidiscrimination framework is overly assimilationist. Relatedly, the second criticism is that the antidiscrimination framework is overly identitarian. Drawing on comparative examples, I will contend that these criticisms ought to inform how—but not whether—SOGI antidiscrimination projects are pursued.

V.A *Critiques Concerning Assimilation*

One progressive critique of antidiscrimination frameworks is that they too often focus on assimilating marginalized groups into existing legal and social institutions and, in so doing, might obscure the possibility of radically transforming the institutions themselves. This critique has been made in a variety of contexts, but has been debated perhaps most hotly with respect to marriage.[179] Thus, this volume will focus its attention on the paradigmatic example of marriage. Before exploring the critique, I will first surface the reasons why many people view same-sex marriage rights to be important.

For many people, extending marriage rights to same-sex couples is crucial because denying same-sex couples the choice to marry perpetuates notions that same-sex couples are somehow inferior to different-sex couples.[180] Granting same-sex couples the freedom to marry represents an acknowledgement that same-sex couples are not second-class citizens. In addition, for many same-sex couples, getting married is a meaningful choice because it expresses the couple's commitment to each other and signals this commitment to the rest of society.[181]

Marriage also carries legal significance. For example, in the United States, thousands of legal provisions distribute rights and responsibilities based on whether a couple is married.[182] The US Supreme Court noted that the government will treat a couple differently, based on whether they are married, for a wide range of issues—"taxation; inheritance and property rights; rules of intestate succession; spousal privilege in the law of evidence; hospital access; medical decision-making authority; adoption rights; the rights and benefits

---

179 For a seminal anti-assimilationist critique regarding marriage, see Paula L. Ettelbrick, "Since When is Marriage a Path to Liberation?," *Out/Look: National Gay & Lesbian Quarterly*, Fall 1989, at 9. For anti-assimilationist critiques with respect to other contexts, see, e.g., Dean Spade, "Under the Cover of Gay Rights," 37 *NYU Review of Law & Social Change* 79, 84–85 (2013).

180 See Suzanne Kim, "Toward Skeptical Marriage Equality," 34 *Harvard Journal of Law & Gender* 37, 49–50 (2011).

181 Id. at 50–51.

182 See Obergefell, supra note 115, at 2601.

of survivors; birth and death certificates; professional ethics rules; campaign finance restrictions; workers' compensation benefits; health insurance; and child custody, support, and visitation rules" just to name a few.[183]

Critics, however, argue that pushing for same-sex marriage diverts attention from law reform that could be more transformative by protecting a broad range of caregiving relationships. For example, one might argue that cohabiting adults who care for each other should have a variety of rights regardless of whether they are married.[184] These rights might range from rights to take time off from work to care for each other during medical emergencies to divorce-like dissolution rights when the relationship ends. Critics also argue that law reform should aim at better protecting individuals who are single.[185] For example, in the United States, many individuals rely on their spouse's employer for health insurance. Commentators have pointed to this health care system as exemplifying the limitations of a legal regime that prioritizes marriage.[186] Focusing on expanding marriage rights arguably risks diverting resources from advocacy efforts to expand access to quality health care to all individuals regardless of relationship status.

Moreover, there are additional philosophical reasons why individuals—gay or straight—may object to marriage.[187] One might oppose the gendered roles and practices that are culturally (if not legally) associated with marriage, especially gendered roles within marriage that subordinate women. One might object to the commercialization of the marriage industry. One might also believe that the culture of marriage is too conformist, the side effect of which is to stigmatize adults who are unmarried. For such philosophical reasons, progressive commentators have critiqued efforts to assimilate same-sex couples into the institution of marriage instead of radically changing the privileged position of marriage in law and society.

Some commentators, however, have argued that marriage rights for same-sex couples need not be mutually exclusive from skepticism toward marriage as an institution.[188] Advocates can push for same-sex couples' marriage rights

---

183 Id.

184 See Kim, supra note 180, at 47.

185 Id.

186 See, e.g., Maxine Eichner, "Marriage and the Elephant: The Liberal Democratic State's Regulation of Intimate Relationships Between Adults," 30 *Harvard Journal of Law & Gender* 25, 55 (2007); Marth Albertson Fineman, *The Autonomy Myth*, at 284–285 (New Press 2004).

187 See Kim, supra note 180, at 47.

188 See, e.g., Kim, supra note 180; Edward Stein, "Marriage or Liberation?: Reflections on Two Strategies in the Struggle for Lesbian and Gay Rights and Relationship Recognition," 61 *Rutgers Law Review* 567 (2009).

while also supporting efforts to protect other family forms, such as civil partnership rights for couples who do not wish to marry. Indeed, the legalization of same-sex marriage might foster a culture of appreciating diverse family forms, which may affect a range of families beyond same-sex couples. As Suzanne Kim put it: "The elimination of the legal barrier to entry into marriage for same-sex couples provides a powerful opportunity to project the value of pluralism."[189] Thus, legalizing same-sex marriage may set the stage for further reforms to family law.

Judicial opinions legalizing same-sex marriage vary in whether they adopt an assimilationist perspective or one that promotes family diversity and pluralism. Juxtaposing the United States' and South Africa's landmark same-sex marriage opinions puts this contrast in sharp relief. Both apex courts held that excluding same-sex couples from marriage is unconstitutional.[190] However, their respective decisions diverged in their conceptualization of marriage.[191]

In the case of *Obergefell v. Hodges*, the US Supreme Court suggested that getting married confers dignity upon people. It stated that marriage "promise[s] nobility and dignity to all persons, without regard to their station in life." It also implied that unmarried individuals are to be pitied. According to *Obergefell*, "Marriage responds to the universal fear that a lonely person might call out only to find no one there."[192] As a result, being unmarried is "be[ing] condemned to live in loneliness, excluded from one of civilization's oldest institutions."[193] *Obergefell* is thus an opinion that centers on assimilating gays and lesbians into the institution of marriage. The opinion does not openly acknowledge the fact that, although marriage is indeed a good choice for many couples, it may not be the right choice for everyone.

In contrast to this uncritical embrace of marriage as an institution, the majority opinion in *Fourie* made clear that it is not marriage *per se* that confers dignity upon couples. Instead, it is the legal right to decide *whether* to marry—and *whether* to marry someone of the same sex—that is central to dignity. While *Fourie* acknowledged that many people find marriage to be extremely meaningful and important,[194] it also openly acknowledged critiques

189 Kim, supra note 180, at 42–46.

190 See Fourie, supra note 174; Obergefell, supra note 115.

191 I have written previously about this comparison at Lau, supra note 168.

192 Obergefell, supra note 115, at 2594. The majority opinion further glorified marriage by stating that "marriage is essential to our most profound hopes and aspirations.... [It is] fulfillment in its highest meaning.... No union is more profound than marriage." Id. at 2594, 2602, 2608.

193 Id. at 2600.

194 Fourie, supra note 174, at paras. 63–72.

of marriage.[195] It recognized that some same-sex couples may reject marriage for philosophical and political reasons.[196] Accordingly, it stated that "what is in issue is not the decision to be taken, but the choice that is available. If heterosexual couples have the option of deciding whether to marry or not, so should same-sex couples have the choice."[197] Rather than denigrate the choice not to marry, the court openly recognized that South Africa has a "multitude of family formations"[198] and is committed to "respect across difference."[199]

Obergefell and *Fourie* illuminate that, in extending marriage rights to same-sex couples, court opinions can diverge in their relationships to anti-assimilationist critiques. By situating dignity interests in the decision whether to marry, as opposed to situating dignity in marriage itself, the majority opinion in *Fourie* avoids the assimilationist undertones of *Obergefell*'s majority opinion.[200]

V.B *Critiques Concerning the Identitarianism Frame*

Some progressive commentators are concerned that LGBT antidiscrimination claims reify socially constructed identity categories in problematic ways.[201] In other words, LGBT antidiscrimination claims rest on the idea that LGBT persons are being treated differently—either directly or indirectly—as compared with straight and cisgender counterparts. Articulating such claims about "LGBT persons" (or subgroups such as gay men or transgender persons) labels people based on their sexual orientation and gender identity. The appropriateness of such labeling has been debated.

The critique about identitarianism is particularly acute where LGBT identity is a relatively new cultural development. For example, individuals who are sexually intimate with members of the same sex do not always form identities around that intimacy by calling oneself "gay," "lesbian," "bisexual," or any

---

195 Id. at para. 72.
196 Id.
197 Id.
198 Id. at para. 59.
199 Id. at para. 60.
200 While I have focused on this case study of same-sex marriage in the United States and South Africa, other commentators have pointed to other examples illustrating that judicial vindication of SOGI nondiscrimination rights can reflect varying degrees of assimilationism. See, e.g., Dickson & Sanders, supra note 160 ("the path of SOGI rights in South Asia forms a counterpoint to the current Western model of legal and social advocacy for LGBT rights, which promotes narratives of similarity and assimilation over those of diversity or the forthright embrace of sexual difference and gender variation.").
201 See supra notes 205–208 and accompanying text.

such identifier.[202] In some parts of the world, thinking about homosexuality in terms of identity is a more recent cultural development than it is in the West.[203] For example, ethnographers have suggested that, until the past two decades or so, individuals in Iran who engaged in same-sex intimacy almost never identified themselves as gay, homosexual, or members of any such identity category.[204] Exploring such recent examples puts in stark relief the cultural contingency of gay identities. There is thus worry about articulating human rights in terms of protecting gay people from discrimination. As scholars such as Jena McGill have noted, requiring an individual to "come out" as gay (or lesbian, bisexual, or transgender) to claim nondiscrimination rights will feel very foreign in places where men who are attracted to men tend not to describe themselves with identity labels based on sexual attraction; moreover, their antidiscrimination claims are unlikely to resonate with the others in their cultural surroundings.[205]

Even in the West, there are concerns about framing rights claims in terms of LGBT identities. Commentators worry that rights movements centered on LGBT identities focus too much on presenting a unified front, essentializing LGBT identities and obscuring diversity within LGBT communities.[206] When such internal diversity is obscured, it is the views and priorities of relatively privileged LGBT persons that may eclipse those of other community members.[207] Commentators have also argued that social and legal reform movements should seek to avoid reifying LGBT identity; instead, the reforms should aim at reducing the social salience of LGBT identities because pigeonholing people into identity categories is stifling.[208]

---

202 See, e.g., Edward O. Laumann et al., *The Social Organization of Sexuality: Sexual Practices in the United States*, at 299 fig. 8.2 (University of Chicago Press 1994).

203 See McGill, supra note 10, at 29–30.

204 See, Pardis Mahdavi, "Questioning the Global Gays(ze): Constructions of Sexual Identities in Post-Revolution Iran," 18 *Social Identities* 223, 225–231 (2012) (presenting ethnographic fieldwork conducted in Iran between 2000 and 2007).

205 McGill, supra note 10, at 29–30 (building on the research of scholars such as Rajesh Dhir, Peter Drucker, Joseph Massad, Hassan El Menyawi, Sonia Katyal, Rosalind Morris, and Shannon Woodcock).

206 For related critiques of LGBT identity politics, see, e.g., Mary Bernstein, "Identity Politics," 31 *Annual Review of Sociology* 47, 56 (2005); Joshua Gamson, "Must Identity Movements Self-Destruct?: A Queer Dilemma," in *Queer Theory Sociology*, at 395, 409–411 (Steven Seidman ed.) (Wiley-Blackwell 1996); Gwendolyn M. Leachman, "Institutionalizing Essentialism: Mechanisms of Intersectional Subordination with the LGBT Movement," 2016 *Wisconsin Law Review* 655 (2016).

207 See Leachman, supra note 206, at 656–661.

208 See Bernstein, supra note 206, at 56; Gamson, supra note 206, at 409–411. In addition to being concerned about identity labels such as "gay" and "lesbian," some commentators

To avoid the identitarian nature of antidiscrimination claims, one might frame rights claims in terms of liberty interests (such as freedom, autonomy, and privacy) as opposed to nondiscrimination. For example, efforts to decriminalize sodomy between men can emphasize the universal right to sexual autonomy, as opposed to gay men's right to nondiscrimination. Likewise, efforts to secure same-sex couples' access to marriage can be framed in terms of the universal freedom to marry, as opposed to gays' and lesbians' right to nondiscrimination.

Asserting these liberty claims alone, without articulating nondiscrimination rights, may well feel unsatisfying.[209] In many parts of the world, people's lived experiences are shaped by SOGI identity categories. To call out and condemn discrimination against minority identity groups has expressive value; vindicating nondiscrimination rights helps destigmatize those groups. Vindication of identity-based antidiscrimination rights may also have valuable precedential effects. For example, when a court strikes down a sodomy law on discrimination grounds, it affirms a nondiscrimination principle that can shape subsequent cases if the jurisdiction adheres to precedents. Courts may later apply that nondiscrimination principle to cases concerning issues such as partnership and marriage rights. In contrast, striking down the law based on privacy grounds may not have the same downstream effects. Identity-based claims have also been a powerful tool for fostering solidarity and mobilization in social justice movements in various parts of the world.[210]

Anti-identitarian critiques of the LGBT nondiscrimination framework can be ameliorated by raising awareness that LGBT identities are diverse and contingent on time and place. Indeed, in the United States, the LGBT rights movement of the 1970s purposefully emphasized internal diversity in its campaigns; it did so to a greater extent than it has in more recent decades.[211] Advocates can recalibrate their campaigns to again more purposefully portray the diversity

---

have raised concerns about elevating the significance of "sexual orientation" and "gender identity" as identity categories. See, e.g., Matthew Waites, "Critique of 'Sexual Orientation' and 'Gender Identity' in Human Rights Discourse: Global Queer Politics Beyond the Yogyakarta Principles," 15 *Contemporary Politics* 137, 143 (2009).

209 For related arguments about the unsatisfactory nature of using non-identitarian claims to advance racial justice, see, e.g., Osamudia R. James, "Valuing Identity," 102 *Minnesota Law Review* 127 (2017).

210 See, e.g., Gamson, supra note 206, at 396 (discussing gay identity politics in the United States); Mahdavi, supra note 204, at 231–234 (describing gay identity politics in Iran).

211 See Leachman, supra note 206, at 670–672, citing Elizabeth A. Armstrong, *Forging Gay Identities: Organizing Sexuality in San Francisco* (University of Chicago Press 2002).

within LGBT communities. Put differently, LGBT rights advocates can avoid essentialism by cultivating a "thinner" construction of LGBT identity.[212]

In earlier writing, I have noted that various interpretations of gay identity have emerged around the world.[213] For example, in Asia, "[b]eing gay has taken on different cultural meanings in places like Mumbai, Hong Kong, Seoul, and Taipei."[214] Exercising agency as informed cultural consumers, local actors have taken notions of gay identity that became popularized in the West and reshaped those identities by injecting them with local cultural sensibilities.[215] Recognizing this hybridity ameliorates concerns that LGBT rights discourse is imperialistic in nature, whereby Western notions of LGBT identity simply displace local cultural conceptions of sexual orientation and gender identity. Some scholars have described this hybridity in terms of a "queer diaspora"[216] to explain that SOGI minorities around the world share commonalities, yet also represent a "contestation of a *unitary* GLBT identity" because the identity varies across the world.[217]

VI Exemptions from SOGI Discrimination Bans

Some of the most high-profile debates about SOGI discrimination protections now center on the question of exemptions: Under what circumstances, if ever, should there be exemptions from SOGI discrimination bans? To some extent, the idea of exemptions seems uncontroversial. Exemptions have long existed, and have gone largely unchallenged, in other realms of discrimination law. For example, it seems relatively uncontroversial to say that churches should be exempt from sex discrimination bans, such that they can refuse to hire female ministers if their religion requires such sex discrimination. Likewise, advocates of SOGI rights usually accept that churches should be exempt from SOGI discrimination bans, such that they can refuse to ordain openly LGBT ministers.

Some controversies concerning exemptions extend across a range of discrimination grounds. For example, there is debate about how broadly to define

212 Daniel Ortiz explained that a "thin" conception of gay identity views gay people as "simply those who experience same-sex desire—no more and no less"; in contrast, a "thick" conception "describes gay people primarily in terms of their social roles and their relationship to other features of social life." Daniel R. Ortiz, "Creating Controversy: Essentialism and Constructivism and the Politics of Gay Identity," 79 *Virginia Law Review* 1833, 1845 (1993).

213 Lau, supra note 156, at 800.

214 Id.

215 Lau, supra note 151, at 523–525.

216 Katyal, supra note 168, at 1429 (building on the works of Simon Watney and others).

217 Id.

what counts as a religious entity for the purpose of ministerial exceptions in employment discrimination law.[218] For example, consider the question: is a teacher employed by a religious school protected by discrimination laws, or is the teacher's position subject to a ministerial exception? This question is relevant regardless of whether the teacher claims that she is discriminated against based on sexual orientation or gender identity, or any other protected category such as sex, race, disability, or religion.

It is beyond the scope of this volume to examine general debates about exemptions that apply across a range of protected categories. Instead, this section will examine two debates that have flared up in the context of SOGI rights, specifically in relation to same-sex marriage. The following section will examine exemptions for civil marriage celebrants who object to officiating same-sex marriages. Afterwards, the next section will examine exemptions for private businesses that invoke religion to justify discrimination. A number of countries around the world have grappled with these areas of dispute. As this volume goes to press, several pieces of pending litigation on such exemptions remain unresolved. Lawyers and scholars who work in the field of SOGI discrimination law are closely following these legal disputes.

VI.A *Exemptions for Civil Marriage Officiants*

As a growing number of jurisdictions extend marriage to same-sex couples, they must grapple with whether to grant exemptions to marriage officiants (also known as marriage celebrants) who object to same-sex marriage on religious grounds. It has been relatively uncontroversial for governments to say that religious ministers are not obligated to officiate same-sex marriages. Greater controversy has surrounded proposals to exempt civil servants who officiate marriages or are otherwise involved in helping couples to marry. In many jurisdictions, government employees—such as clerks, registrars, judges, and magistrates—have job duties that include involvement in marriage proceedings.[219] There have been heated debates over granting these civil servants the ability to refuse providing their government services to same-sex couples based on their religious beliefs. Indeed, some jurisdictions have passed laws to grant such exemptions to civil servants. Notably, these civil servants do

---

218 See generally Pamela Slotte & Helge Årsheim, "The Ministerial Exception—Comparative Perspectives," 4 *Oxford Journal of Law and Religion* 171 (2015).

219 Civil servants are sometimes involved in marriage proceedings even if they do not officiate the marriage. For example, in the United States, one civil servant (e.g., a clerk) may be responsible for processing a couple's marriage license and then another civil servant (e.g., a judge) may be responsible for officiating (also known as solemnizing) the marriage. In this section of the volume, however, I will focus on the paradigmatic case of civil marriage officiants.

not work for a religious entity, nor are they acting in any official religious capacity when they officiate marriages. Yet the exemptions allow them to recuse themselves from serving same-sex couples who seek civil marriage.

To be sure, many jurisdictions have debated and then rejected the idea of granting civil marriage officiants exemptions. The national governments of New Zealand and the United Kingdom are recent examples.[220] In some other jurisdictions, laws have been created to exempt civil servants. One type of exemption system allows civil servants to refuse to provide same-sex couples with marriage-related services while continuing to service different-sex couples. This system has been adopted in a range of jurisdictions, including the Netherlands, South Africa, and the states of Mississippi and Utah in the United States.

The Netherlands was the first county in the world to legalize same-sex marriage. Dutch lawmakers legalized same-sex marriage without being ordered to do so by a constitutional court, and allowing exemption for civil servants was a pragmatic compromise.[221] Although the exemptions were once widely supported by the Dutch public, over time, there was growing criticism that the exemptions were unfair toward same-sex couples.[222] In 2014, the Dutch legislature passed a law to preclude any new civil marriage officiants from receiving an exemption.[223]

In South Africa, the Constitutional Court was the first national apex court to hold that depriving same-sex couples of marriage is unconstitutional.[224] The Court, however, did not order the government to register same-sex marriages right away. Instead, the Court gave the South African Parliament one year to finalize legislative reform to legalize same-sex marriage.[225] As a result, Parliament passed legislation that extended marriage rights to same-sex couples, but also granted civil servants an exemption if they object to performing

---

220 See Stijn Smet, "The Problem of a Same Sex Marriage Exemption for Civil Celebrants," *Pursuit*, 29 November 2017, pursuit.unimelb.edu.au/articles/the-problem-of-a-same-sex-marriage-exemption-for-civil-celebrants.

221 See Stijn Smet, "Conscientious Objection to Same-sex Marriages: Beyond the Limits of Toleration," 11 *Religion & Human Rights* 114 (2016).

222 Id.

223 Id. at 116, citing Wet van 4 juli 2014 tot wijziging van het Burgerlijk Wetboek en de Algemene wet gelijke behandeling met betrekking tot ambtenaren van de burgerlijke stand die onderscheid maken als bedoeld in de Algemene wetgelijke behandeling [Act of 4 July 2014 amending the Civil Code and the General Act on equal treatment, with regards to civil servants who treat persons differently in terms of the General Act on equal treatment], Staatsblad 2014 260.

224 See Fourie, supra note 174, at para. 114.

225 Id.

same-sex marriages based on conscience.[226] The president's office eventually signed this law into effect. Scholars and LGBT rights advocates have criticized South Africa's exemptions for civil marriage officials for being unconstitutional, arguing that the exemptions impermissibly discriminate against same-sex couples.[227] Advocates have not, however, challenged the exemptions in court because they have chosen to devote their limited resources to other issues, such as combatting hate crimes.[228]

Meanwhile, advocates have in fact chosen to challenge the exemptions for civil marriage officiants in Mississippi.[229] The state of Mississippi created an exemption for civil marriage officiants after the US Supreme Court's decision in *Obergefell* led to the legalization of same-sex marriage in that state.[230] At the time of writing this volume, the litigation in Mississippi is still pending.[231] Like Mississippi, the state of Utah also allows government employees to exempt themselves from performing same-sex marriages.[232] It is worth noting that the

---

226 See Civil Union Act 17 of 2006, Sec. 6. For an elaboration on the compromise embodied by the Civil Union Act, see David Bilchitz with Melanie Judge, "The Civil Union Act: Messy Compromise or Giant Leap Forward?," in *To Have and To Hold: The Making of Same-Sex Marriage in South Africa*, at 149 (Melanie Judge et al. eds.) (Jacana Media 2009); Lau, supra note 116, at 300–301.

227 E.g., Pierre de Vos, "The 'Inevitability' of Same-Sex Marriage in South Africa's Post-Apartheid State," 23 *South African Journal on Human Rights* 432, 463 (2007).

228 See Lau, supra note 116, at 300.

229 See Zakiya Summers, "ACLU of MS Responds to Supreme Court's Refusal to Hear HB 1523 Challenge," ACLU of Mississippi, 9 January 2018, www.aclu-ms.org/en/news/aclu-ms-responds-supreme-courts-refusal-hear-hb-1523-challenge.

230 Mississippi's exemptions for civil marriage officiants is embedded in a law that also provides legal immunity to other actors (e.g., businesses, landlords, adoption agencies) that discriminate based on religious or moral opposition to same-sex marriage. See Protecting Freedom of Conscience from Government Discrimination Act (commonly referred to as HB 1523), Ch. 334, 2016 Miss. Laws 427 (codified at Miss. Code Ann. Secs. 11-62-1 to -19 (2017)). See also Mark Joseph Stern, "Mississippi's Uniquely Cruel Anti-LGBTQ Law May Be Heading to the Supreme Court," *Slate*, 2 October 2017, 1:40 PM, www.slate.com/blogs/outward/2017/10/02/mississippi_s_hb_1523_may_be_heading_to_the_supreme_court.html (describing Mississippi's law as "a direct response to Obergefell….").

231 The US Supreme Court has declined to review an appellate court ruling that plaintiffs lacked standing to challenge Mississippi's religious exemptions law, HB 1523. The ACLU of Mississippi has stated, however, they intend to proceed with their narrower lawsuit that challenges only the portion of HB 1523 that concerns civil marriage officiants. See Summers, supra note 229.

232 Protections for Religious Expression and Beliefs about Marriage, Family, or Sexuality, 2015 Utah S.B. 297, codified as Utah Code Ann. 1953 Secs. 17-20-4, 30-1-6, 63G-20-103, 63G-20-202 (West 2015). See also Nicholas J. Schilling Jr., "Analysis of Statutory Religious Accommodations for State-Employed Religious Objectors to Same-sex Marriage Solemnization," 31 *Notre Dame Journal of Law, Ethics & Public Policy* 431, 448–450 (2017).

laws in Mississippi and Utah both require government offices to ensure that all same-sex couples who seek to marry are able to do so despite the recusal of individual civil officiants.[233]

The state of North Carolina allows government employees to recuse themselves from performing same-sex marriages if doing so conflicts with their sincerely held religious beliefs.[234] North Carolina also requires that there is someone within each local jurisdiction of North Carolina who is willing to perform same-sex marriages.[235] North Carolina's situation differs from that of Mississippi and Utah in at least two ways. First, government officials in North Carolina cannot choose to recuse themselves from performing same-sex marriages alone. Instead, they must recuse themselves from performing all marriages.[236] For example, magistrate judges are authorized to serve as celebrants in North Carolina; if a judge wishes to recuse herself from performing same-sex marriages, she must recuse herself from performing all marriages. The judge would continue to oversee other judicial matters, but would not officiate any marriages. Second, North Carolina differs from Mississippi and Utah because it allows civil servants to be exempt from performing any type of marriage based on religious beliefs, not only same-sex marriages.[237] Thus, a magistrate judge who holds a religious objection to interracial marriages may recuse herself from officiating all marriages. These two aspects of North Carolina's law ameliorate some of the discriminatory aspects of other exemptions schemes. Critics, however, still contend that North Carolina's exemption system is discriminatory, relegating same-sex couples to second-class citizenship.[238]

---

233 Utah's law requires each county in Utah to ensure that someone is available in the county to perform legal marriages for same-sex couples; this person may be a government employee or religious celebrant to whom the county can refer same-sex couples. See Schilling, supra note 232, at 449. The Mississippi law requires relevant government entities to ensure that authorization, licensing, solemnization, and performance "of any legally valid marriage is not impeded or delayed as a result of any recusal." Miss. Code Ann. Sec. 11-62-5(8)(a)–(b).

234 An Act to Allow Magistrates, Assistant Registers of Deeds, and Deputy Registers of Deeds to Recuse Themselves From Performing Duties Related to Marriage Ceremonies Due to Sincerely Held Religious Objection (commonly referred to as SB2), 2015 N.C. Session Law 75. See also Schilling, supra note 232, at 446–448.

235 See Schilling, supra note 232, at 447–448.

236 Id. at 447.

237 Id. at 446.

238 See "Anti-LGBT Bill SB2 Becomes Law in NC," *Campaign for Southern Equality*, southernequality.org/sb2-becomes-law-in-nc. Advocates have sued to challenge the constitutionality of SB2, but courts have ruled that plaintiffs in the lawsuit lacked standing. Ansley v. Warren, No. 1:16-cv-00054, 2016 WL 5213937 (W.D.N.C., 20 September 2016), affirmed by 861 F.3d 512 (4th Cir. 2017). See also "Plaintiffs respond to 4th Circuit ruling on SB2, North

Some jurisdictions have sought to strike compromises through what can be termed "grandfather clauses." For example, when the Netherlands passed legislation to eliminate exemptions for civil marriage celebrants, the elimination of exemptions only applied to new civil celebrants.[239] Civil celebrants who had already been granted exemptions were allowed to retain those exemptions. Similarly, Australia's marriage equality legislation created a grandfather clause. When Australia legalized same-sex marriage, the government allowed existing civil celebrants to become classified as "religious celebrants" who are exempt from performing same-sex marriages for religious reasons, even though they are not religious ministers.[240] This classification, however, was only available to existing civil celebrants.[241] Going forward, religious exemptions in Australia will only be granted to religious ministers, as opposed to lay persons who object to same-sex marriage for religious reasons.

VI.B *Exemptions for Businesses*

Another hotly debated issue is the appropriateness of granting exemptions to private businesses that wish to discriminate based on sexual orientation for religious reasons. This section will examine developments in two jurisdictions—the United States and the United Kingdom—where this issue remains unsettled and is quickly evolving.

In the United States, the recently decided Supreme Court case of *Masterpiece Cakeshop v. Colorado Civil Rights Commission* has garnered widespread attention.[242] The case concerned a bakery in Colorado named Masterpiece Cakeshop, which refused to design and create a wedding cake for two men because of the owner's religious opposition to same-sex marriage.[243] The two men, Charlie Craig and Dave Mullins, argued that the bakery's refusal of service violated the Colorado Anti-Discrimination Act,[244] which prohibits businesses

---

Carolina 'Magistrate Recusal' Law," *Campaign for Southern Equality*, southernequality.org/plaintiffs-respond-4th-circuit-ruling-sb2-north-carolina-magistrate-recusal-law.

239 See Smet, supra note 221, at 130.

240 "Marriage Equality in Australia," Australian Government Attorney-General's Department, www.ag.gov.au/marriageequality. For background information about Australia's civil marriage celebrant system, see Becky Batagol, "Why There Should Be No Room in the Law for Celebrants to Discriminate on Same-sex Marriage," *Conversation*, 17 November 2017, theconversation.com/why-there-should-be-no-room-in-the-law-for-celebrants-to-discriminate-on-same-sex-marriage-87590.

241 "Marriage Equality in Australia," supra note 240.

242 Masterpiece Cakeshop v. Colorado Civil Rights Commission, 584 U.S. __ (2018) (slip opinion).

243 Id. at 3–4.

244 Colorado Anti-Discrimination Act (CADA), Secs. 24-34-301 to -804, CRS 2014.

from discriminating based on sexual orientation. In response, the bakery's owner, Jack Phillips, countered that enforcing the nondiscrimination provision against him would violate his constitutional freedom of religion. He also argued that any state action requiring him to create the cake would violate his constitutional right to free expression by forcing him to express support for same-sex marriage. In essence, the baker claimed an exemption from the Colorado Anti-Discrimination Act. The Colorado Civil Rights Commission and the Colorado Court of Appeal both ruled in favor of the same-sex couple.[245] The Supreme Court, however, reversed in favor of the baker on very narrow grounds, leaving unresolved larger questions about whether businesses can be exempt from laws that prohibit sexual orientation discrimination.[246]

The Supreme Court's decision in *Masterpiece Cakeshop* hinged on circumstances that were very specific to the case. According to the Court, the Colorado Civil Rights Commission's consideration of this case was marred by "a clear and impermissible hostility" toward Mr. Phillips' sincere religious beliefs.[247] For example, the Court noted that one Commissioner disparaged Mr. Phillips' religious position by calling it "one of the most despicable pieces of rhetoric that people can use."[248] The Court ultimately concluded that the Commission deprived Mr. Phillips of an impartial hearing in violation of his right to free religious exercise. The Court emphasized, however, that cases with facts similar to *Masterpiece Cakeshop* may well reach a different outcome if they are not marred by the procedural flaws in *Masterpiece Cakeshop*.[249] Indeed, the majority opinion contained soaring dicta suggesting that businesses usually should not be permitted to invoke religion to excuse themselves from discrimination laws. The Court noted that it is appropriate to exempt clergy, so that they are not compelled to perform marriage ceremonies for same-sex couples, but exemptions ought to be confined: "it is a general rule that such [religious and philosophical] objections do not allow business owners and other actors in the economy and in society to deny protected persons equal access to goods and services."[250] Within days after the Supreme Court handed down its decision, a state court in Arizona cited the dicta in *Masterpiece Cakeshop* to support its ruling that a business selling wedding stationary and décor may not

245 See Masterpiece Cakeshop, supra note 242, at 8–9.
246 Id. at 18.
247 Id. at 12.
248 Id. at 13–14.
249 Id. at 18.
250 Id. at 9.

invoke religion to reject clients based on sexual orientation.[251] Advocates and scholars are watching closely to see whether more courts will eventually cite *Masterpiece Cakeshop* as this Arizona court has.

Across the Atlantic, another case involving a cake shop is still pending.[252] The Northern Ireland case of *Lee v. McArthur and Ashers Baking Company Limited* concerns a gay man, Gareth Lee, who ordered a cake from Ashers Bakery. He requested that the cake bear the logo of an LGBT organization and the slogan "Support Gay Marriage." The owners of the bakery, Mr. and Mrs. McArthur, cancelled the order and refunded Mr. Lee his deposit. Based on their religious beliefs, they stated that they oppose same-sex marriage and the prospect of its legalization in Northern Ireland. The county court and Northern Ireland Court of Appeal both sided with Mr. Lee, ruling that the bakery violated Northern Ireland's laws[253] prohibiting discrimination based on sexual orientation as well as political opinion. Although Mr. Lee was not discriminated against based on his personal sexual orientation, the slogan he requested is associated with homosexuality and, thus, the case involved associative discrimination based on sexual orientation. The McArthurs argued that requiring them to make the cake would violate their rights to religion and free expression enshrined in the European Convention of Human Rights, but courts thus far have rejected those contentions. *McArthur v. Lee* is now pending before the UK Supreme Court.

It is worth noting that the Northern Ireland Court of Appeal had relied in part on the earlier UK Supreme Court case of *Bull v. Hall*, which will likely influence the Supreme Court's deliberation on the pending bakery case.[254] In *Bull v. Hall*, the Supreme Court ruled that a pair of hotel owners could not justify discrimination against a same-sex couple based on the owners' religious beliefs. The Supreme Court held that prohibiting the hotel owners from discrimination did not disproportionately restrict the hotel owners' freedom of religion.

The cases from the United States and the United Kingdom highlight how the law concerning religious exemptions is still under development.[255] Ongoing disputes in this area of law may ultimately affect not only sexual orientation

---

251 See Brush & Nib Studio v. City of Phoenix, Arizona Court of Appeals, No. CV2016-05225, 7 June 2018 (bench opinion).

252 See Lee v. McArthur, [2016] NICA (Civ), at 5 (Northern Ireland).

253 Equality Act (Sexual Orientation Regulations) 2006 (Northern Ireland); Fair Employment and Treatment Order 1998 (Northern Ireland).

254 Bull v. Hall [2013] UKSC 73.

255 Lower courts in other countries have also been grappling with this issue. For a discussion of related cases from Canada and Australia, as well the United States and the United

discrimination but discrimination on other grounds as well. For example, if the UK Supreme Court rules that Ashers Bakery is exempt for religious reasons, it may pave the way for other businesses to refuse providing wedding-related services based on religious objections not only to same-sex marriage, but also other types of marriage. For instance, a wedding caterer might invoke religious objections to refuse providing services to an interfaith couple or an interracial couple. Indeed, pending court cases about religious exemptions raise the specter of widely opening the door to exemptions, which is a cause of concern for equality advocates.

Conclusion

This volume has examined five major questions concerning the development of SOGI discrimination law: (1) Is SOGI discrimination encompassed by existing laws that prohibit discrimination based on sex? (2) Should sexual orientation and gender identity be considered protected categories in and of themselves? (3) Is there a standard sequence for developing legal protections against SOGI discrimination? (4) What are the drawbacks of developing SOGI discrimination protections? (5) To what extent should religious objections justify exemptions from SOGI discrimination bans?

There are numerous benefits to approaching these questions from a comparative perspective. First, there is value in cross-fertilization of ideas. For example, although the UN Human Rights Committee stated early on that sexual orientation discrimination is a form of sex discrimination, domestic courts—especially in the United States—subsequently developed the logical underpinnings of that claim. Comparative analysis also illuminates competing approaches to SOGI issues. For instance, jurisdictions that are grappling with the question of same-sex marriage can see, through comparative analysis, that there is more than one way to legalize same-sex marriage. Different countries have taken different approaches with potentially different downstream effects. Comparative study of SOGI discrimination is also useful because looking abroad can help to unsettle certain assumptions that may hinder domestic deliberations on SOGI discrimination rights. For example, studying South Asian jurisprudence that recognizes a third sex might help to unsettle assumptions within other jurisdictions that binary male/female categories are natural as opposed to social constructs.

Kingdom, see Mel Cousins, "Sexual Orientation, Equal Treatment and the Right to Manifest Religion: Lee v McArthur," 28 *King's Law Journal* 425, 436–441 (2017).

Indeed, comparative study of SOGI discrimination is fruitful in a variety of ways. The short list of ways provided here is not intended to be exhaustive. Indeed this volume serves as a springboard for further research and discussion about comparative SOGI discrimination law.

Acknowledgement

Thank you to Barbara Fedders and Kendall Simms for their assistance during the writing of this volume.

References

Hunter, Nan D., "The Sex Discrimination Argument in Gay Rights Cases," 9 *Journal of Law & Policy* 397 (2001).

Inter-American Commission on Human Rights, *Violence Against LGBTI Persons* (2015).

Katyal, Sonia, "The Dissident Citizen," 57 *UCLA Law Review* 1415 (2010).

Kim, Suzanne A., "Skeptical Marriage Equality," 34 *Harvard Journal of Law & Gender* 37 (2012).

Lau, Holning, "Grounding Conversations on Sexuality and Asian Law," 44 *U.C. Davis Law Review* 773 (2011).

Lau, Holning, "Marriage Equality and Family Diversity: Comparative Perspectives from the United States and South Africa," 85 *Fordham Law Review* 2615 (2017).

McGill, Jena, "SOGI.... So What: Sexual Orientation, Gender Identity and Human Rights Discourse at the United Nations," 3 *Canadian Journal of Human Rights* 1 (2014).

McGoldrick, Dominic, "The Development and Status of Sexual Orientation Discrimination under International Human Rights Law," 16 *Human Rights Law Review* 613 (2016).

Merin, Yuval, *Equality for Same-Sex Couples: The Legal Recognition of Gay Partnerships in Europe and the United States* (University of Chicago Press 2012).

Minter, Shannon, "Do Transsexuals Dream of Gay Rights? Getting Real about Transgender Inclusion in the Gay Rights Movement," 17 *New York Law School Journal of Human Rights* 589 (2000–2001).

Muntarbhorn, Vitit, *Protection Against Violence and Discrimination Based on Sexual Orientation and Gender Identity*, United Nations General Assembly, Doc. A/72/172, 19 July 2017.

O'Flaherty, Martin & John Fisher, "Sexual Orientation, Gender Identity and International Human Rights Law: Contextualising the Yogyakarta Principles," 8 *Human Rights Law Review* 207 (2008).

Raub, Amy, Adele Cassola, Isabel Latz & Jody Heymann, "Protections of Equal Rights across Sexual Orientation and Gender Identity: An Analysis of 193 National Constitutions," 28 *Yale Journal of Law & Feminism* 149 (2016).

Spade, Dean, "Under the Cover of Gay Rights," 37 *NYU Review of Law & Social Change* 79 (2013).

Stein, Edward, "Immutability and Innateness Arguments About Lesbian, Gay, and Bisexual Rights," 89 *Chicago-Kent Law Review* 597 (2014).

Wintemute, Robert, *Sexual Orientation and Human Rights: The United States Constitution, the European Convention, and the Canadian Charter* (Clarendon Press 1997).

Other Titles in Comparative Discrimination Law

Comparative Discrimination Law: Historical and Theoretical Frameworks

Laura Carlson ISBN 9789004345447

Human history is marked by group and individual struggles for emancipation, equality and self-expression. This first volume in the *Brill Research Perspectives in Comparative Discrimination Law* briefly explores some of the history underlying these efforts in the field of discrimination law. A broad discussion of the historical development of issues of discrimination is first set out, looking at certain international, regional and national bases for modern discrimination legal structures. Several of the theoretical frameworks invoked in a comparative discrimination law analysis are then addressed, either as institutional frameworks or theories addressing specific protection grounds. This first volume is dedicated to setting out an introduction to the field of comparative discrimination law to give the reader a platform from which to undertake further reading and research in the compelling topic of comparative discrimination law.

International Human Rights Law and Discrimination Protections; A Comparison of Regional and National Responses

Mpoki Mwakagali ISBN 9789004345461

Non-discrimination is a fundamental principle of international human rights law. This volume discusses the international legal framework on this principle and comparatively elaborates the definition of discrimination as well as the grounds of discrimination in the various general and specialised international human rights treaties, including the International Labour Organisation conventions. The element of special measures as an integral aspect of this principle is also raised. A comparative discussion on the incorporation of international standards on the principle of non-discrimination established in the international treaties in regional as well as national human rights frameworks is also set forth to provide practical illustrations of the application of these standards in more specific and localised perspectives. Selected regional frameworks discussed are the African, American and European human rights regional frameworks and the national frameworks are South Africa and Brazil.

Comparative Discrimination Law; Age as a Protected Ground

Lucy Vickers ISBN 9789004345539

This comparative review of age as a protected ground in discrimination law explores the underpinning questions and themes related to two main dimensions of age discrimination. The first dimension is structural, economic and labour market driven, whereby age is used to allocate a range of rights, obligations and benefits within society. The second is the social justice and equality dimension, in which age is understood as an aspect of individual identity that is worthy of protection against indignity or detriment. The review then considers the law on age discrimination in a number of jurisdictions, the EU law, the UK, Sweden, USA, Canada and South Africa, and assesses the extent to which the underpinning questions explain the developing case law.

Print Book Orders and Journal Subscription

Customers outside the Americas

BRILL
c/o Turpin Distribution
Stratton Business Park
Pegasus Drive
Biggleswade
Bedfordshire SG18 8TQ
United Kingdom
T +44 (0) 1767 604-954
F +44 (0) 1767 601-640
brill@turpin-distribution.com

Customers in the Americas

BRILL
c/o Turpin Distribution
143 West Street
New Milford, CT 06776
United States
T (844) 232 3707 (Toll free US and Canada)
T +1 (860) 350 0041
F +1 (860) 350 0039
brillna@turpin-distribution.com

Online Resources and Primary Sources

Customers outside the Americas

BRILL
P.O. Box 9000
2300 PA Leiden
The Netherlands
T +31 (0)71-53 53 500
F +31 (0)71-53 17 532
sales-nl@brill.com

Customers in the Americas

BRILL
2 Liberty Square, 11th Floor
Boston, MA 02109
United States
T 1-617-263-2323
F 1-617-263-2324
sales-us@brill.com

www.ingramcontent.com/pod-product-compliance
Lightning Source LLC
Chambersburg PA
CBHW031334230926
51848CB00001B/225